BELIEVE
IF I CAN, YOU CAN

CASSANDRA HOUSE

Authorsunite.com

"You know there are so many people out there that teach the laws of success, teach the science of success, and teach the power of believing. But there are very few people that have not only learned it, but also applied it in their lives and shown other people how to succeed with these very principles. Cassandra House is one of those individuals that has done it! She's done it in her own personal life, she's done it in her business life and now she's reaching back to the rest of the world to teach and to inspire them so that they too can know, that if she can do it, that they can do it too! This is a must-read for anyone who wants to take their lives to the next level and take their belief system to heights that they never thought could ever happen. Read it!"

–Dr David Imonitie, World Renowned
Leader, Coach, and Entrepreneur

When I think of Cassandra I think of heart. She's all heart. She's a giver, a leader and the kind of person that makes you feel invincible in her presence. **In this book, she loves and believes in you with her whole heart.**"

–Debbie Neal, Award Winning Business
Leader and Keynote Speaker

"This is more than a book, it's a tool to **unlock every ounce of self-belief** so you can achieve your greatest potential."

–Kim Mellor, Manifestation
Coach, Leader and Podcaster

"There is something truly unique about her. She has an incredible gift of developing individuals to dig deep into their belief systems and help them move forward in pursuit of their wildest dreams! To be around her is a privilege and now the world gets to hear her genius in this book following her success principles to take themselves to the next level!"

–Gillian Hourihan, TV Producer, Speaker, and Leader

"Cassandra has a true gift when it comes to breathing belief into others. **This book is the next-best thing to being mentored by her one-on-one.** This is an invaluable guide to help you get from where you are to where you want to be in life."

–Emily Swaffield, Health Coach, Mentor, and Speaker

CONTENTS

To get the most out of this book, get a pen and journal so you can complete each challenge found at the end of each chapter.

Doing so will take what you learn from your head to your heart. When you get to the quote page after each challenge, please read it with full belief out loud, look in the mirror or read it to yourself. Let it sink in and fully embrace what it says; let it be true for you.

I also encourage you to read this book along with my course,

21 Days to Believing in Yourself

A lesson a day for the first 21 days of your journey with me will take you to new heights of BELIEVING.

Access your gift from me here.

www.cassandrahouse.com/21days

Code: GIFT21

I Love you and I BELIEVE in YOU!

ACKNOWLEDGMENTS

This year marks my twentieth anniversary as a teacher, coach, educator, and mentor. In this time, there have been so many who have supported, taught, and guided me along my journey. This book is a reflection of everything I have learned from all of them as well as the personal experiences I have gathered along the way. If there is something that I can always promise, it is that I will only ever share what I know to be true, tried, tested, and result-producing. I will never teach you anything that I haven't implemented in my life over and over myself. These are all things that have brought me consistent success. Treat my example as 'results 101.' You deserve to see the fruits of your believing in all the areas of your life as I have.

So, I just want to thank you–wherever you are in the world–for celebrating this accomplishment with me. If you are reading this, you are my people. I want to send love to all my students, past and present, young and old. I see you living your bright, amazing lives and chasing after all the things you love and believe in.

To my clients who have always been there to support me in all of my business ventures, I want to offer my heartfelt thanks. To those I have trained to have their own businesses, schools, studios, and beyond, I am so proud of you. You are a team of life changers and on-fire leaders. I love you like family.

To my mentors, coaches, and teachers that made me the mentor, coach, and teacher I am today, I am forever indebted to you and am grateful to you all, forever.

To my Grandparents on both sides John and Betty House, Shirley and Arthur Whyms. You have each contributed so much to who and what I am today. I have been so blessed to have had all four of you in my life until recently. I am still so blessed to have my two precious Nanna's to love. This week when I rang you both to tell you that I was writing my first book, it felt so special to hear your voices and words of belief flow into me. You are two of the most powerful, loving, spiritual, strong women I have ever known. To my incredible uncles, aunties, and cousins, oh the dinner parties, trips, fun, and laughter we have all had together! I am so glad we all have the travel bug so we can meet up and make memories all over the world. The entrepreneurial blood from you all runs thick, and it is the inspiration from you all to keep the family traditions and our creative spirits alive, that fuels me. Always having and hearing all your new ideas and ventures on the go makes me level up and go for it each day. Something fun is always happening somewhere in this family.

Especially to my father James, mother Deborah, and brother Dorian, I want to thank you for always believing in and investing in me. Because of your support, I have had the opportunity to become the best version of myself and do what I love. I think of your wisdom daily. I am who I am because of you three. Endless and grateful love to you always. Dad, if you remember when I was a little girl with massive dreams, I used to run up the hallway and break a hard left turn into your office. I'd usually say, "Dad, what about this idea?" You would always listen and reply, "Well, if you think you can, you can." That is something you still say to this day, and it is the greatest gift ever. Mum, you always used to say, "Darling, you're beautiful and gorgeous, and yes, you can do anything you put your mind to," always said with oh such grace. That always fueled me with self-belief like you would never know. Dorian, you may be three years younger than me, but you're like the big brother I never had. I've always wished I could be as cool as you. You've been an inspiration and have helped me through everything. You are just the best (and you're still way cooler than me). We will always be the House Family from Kingsley St, Byron Bay, Australia. To the community and town that nurtured and held the breeding ground for incredible moments, memories, and family experiences I loved it all. You were the best foundation a girl could ever ask for. As I travel the globe you are always home and I hold a special place in my heart for all those childhood memories always. Finally, let's not forget Paddington House: our main man. Our doggy that makes the world go 'round (when people talk about their dogs in books, I'm always like, "Really?" But now I'm that person. I get it, and I am loving every second of it.).

So, here's to the next twenty years and beyond. I know the best is yet to come.

Believe: If I can, you can.

1

YOUR FUTURE AWAITS

I encourage you to find somewhere calm, cozy, and relaxing as you embark on this first chapter with me. Picture this:

As you're sitting in your chair, you see a light beam shooting down to the left of where you are, piercing into the ground. You are transfixed by this light beam, and as you continue to look at it, you take hold of it with your hand and start to float up. As you ascend, you see your room getting smaller and smaller—your street, your suburb, and your town below getting further out of sight. As you look around, you see that you are floating up, up, up into the thick, velvety sky. You see your state, country, and the globe becoming a radiant sphere. As you travel past the clouds and into the stars, you feel nurtured and supported by the magnitude around you. When you reach the highest point, you notice another light beam shooting down on the right-hand side of you that begins to pierce the globe below in a new location you have never visited before. You take hold of this new light beam and trust your new direction to float all the way back down. You sail past the stars, through the clouds until you see the outline of your country, your state, your town, and a street where you will land. You float cautiously and gently down to land safely back on planet Earth.

When you stand up from your chair, you find that you're standing on the front lawn of the most beautiful house that you have ever seen. Its appearance and layout are already as familiar to you as the lines on your hands, yet you are pretty sure that you have never been here before. You recognize this place because it is your dream home–the home where your Future Self lives. You know the one: the house that you always picture yourself in when you imagine your future; the one that's made it onto countless vision boards and into many a daydream. The perfect ideal of your dream home has suddenly been made real in its most gorgeous, shining form and you have found yourself on its very doorstep.

As you raise your hand to knock on the door, you can already hear footsteps coming towards you. When the door opens, you are greeted by someone even more familiar than the house itself. Their resemblance to you is uncanny, and the similarities in their demeanor are instantly recognizable. Their appearance is one that only you could possibly know, yet not something you could begin to describe. If you were to take a guess, you might at first think that they are You, but with all that you desire for yourself on this journey. The idea in and of itself is at once both amusing and surreal. It seems impossible, yet at the same time, you see them as they are (as you want to see yourself in the future) and they smile and reach out to hug you. You open wide for a grand, welcoming hug.

Who is this person?

They are your highest, truest, grandest vision for what you desire to become.

They are you, five years from now.

"Welcome," they say. "This is where we live now."

The feeling is awe-inspiring; comforting yet filled with a deep internal knowing. You're reassured that you really have become the best version of yourself.

You take a moment to observe their perfection, their glowing skin, the shape of their face, their style of hair, jewelry and watch.

You note the perfume or cologne are they wearing. You notice the cut of their clothes. You admire the colors. You take it all in. This is the ultimate and imperfectly perfect you. Take them all in, their essence, their energy, their poise and demeanor. After all, it is you.

It's real and it's you.

It's all perfect.

All is welcome and that's all that matters.

As you enter, you are struck by the electric, abundant, and pure energy in the house. The scent inside is perfect and the decor is exactly what you would have picked if this house were yours. As you follow your future self into the main part of the house, walking behind them, you take a moment to notice how do you feel. How do they walk, move, and own the space around them? What is the beautiful area you have entered in the home like? All at once, you are reminded that this house *is* yours, and your only repeating thought is,

"Wow. It actually happened. I actually live here. I did it."

At this moment, your Future Self offers you whatever you want to drink (of course all your favorites are on hand. It's your house, after all; it is you.) and they invite you to sit with them in the living room. As you have a seat on your dream couch, you take a moment to look around and take it all in. After a while, your Future Self joins you again and offers you your drink (I would be having a glass of crisp, chilled champagne in my favorite flute of course. But as for yours, you decide). As you hold your drink for a moment, it is completely quiet. Not awkward, just contemplative. After a few moments of complete contentment, your Future Self says,

"I am here to help you. You can ask me three questions."

Of course, in your excitement, your replies come rapid-fire and without hesitation:

(1) "What do I need to do differently right now to make sure this version of me becomes true? (2) What do I need to give up to have this life? (3) What is one piece of advice you would like to give me, your Younger Self?"

"Is that all you'd like to ask?" says your Future Self. "For the sake of abundance, is there anything else? You can ask me one last question."

At this, you experience a familiar gut feeling; the one where you know you would love to ask just one specific thing that you have on your mind and heart. What is *your* fourth question? I urge you here to imagine sitting on this couch across from your Future Self. As you ask these four questions, just let the answers flow to you. Trust me, the answers will come. Just sit, breathe, and give it time.

As you continue to read this book, keep these questions and the answers you received at the forefront of your mind. Who knows? You might have already had a vivid idea of what your Future Self would be like. Maybe they've accomplished something you constantly dream about but have thought is impossible. If so, you've already seen it in the house as true and achieved.

Now ask yourself this:

How many times have you had a dream and let it fall by the wayside? Have you ever had an idea that felt as if it was not just any ordinary dream? One of those all-consuming, butterflies-in-your-stomach, capital "D" Dreams? Yet, despite all your greatest ambitions and aspirations, a little voice in your head always seems to whisper in reply, "You could never do that!"

When you heard the answers from your Future Self, you may have wondered, where did all the strength and knowing come from? It came from you. You are your greatest source of wisdom and knowledge. Your inner guidance and intuition have been with you all along. We spend so much time asking for advice, Googling what to do, how to do it, and wondering about the answers to our big Q's. However, guess what? The answers are all within you. They have been all along. Trust your truest, highest, grandest vision you hold for yourself, your stunning and incredible Future Self.

They are there for you to connect with at any time.

Get your pen and paper and start writing the vision you experienced.

Detail everything as a letter to yourself of exactly what your visualization was like.

About the house, your future self, all the details. Leave nothing out.

Write it out as a future vision to yourself and read it each night before you go to bed to further imprint it into your subconscious mind.

Next:

Write the Answers you received to the questions you just asked.

1. What do I need to do differently right now to make sure this version of me becomes true?
2. What do I need to give up to live this life?
3. What is one piece of advice you would like to give me, your Younger Self?"
4. What is your fourth question, that last and final question that was on your heart?

I am creating a reality where I am living the highest, truest, grandest, VISION I hold for myself!

2

GIVE YOURSELF RADICAL PERMISSION

Have you ever felt that you were made for more? That you are in possession of enormous potential? Have you felt a deep knowing that if you were watered and cultivated, you would absolutely blossom into greatness? Despite this, the cycle of watching and waiting to be ready has left you in what feels like an unbreakable loop.

If any of this resonates with you, I am so glad that you found this book.

From this moment forward, I want you to allow me to be your human-sized permission slip to believe in yourself, until you fully, utterly, and unapologetically ready to believe in yourself. This process begins with you giving yourself *radical permission* to do so. This means if you have a thought, an idea, or creative burst, before that ever-familiar voice can naysay you out of it, I want you to tell yourself:

I am made for this. My dreams matter. I am going to believe in myself and follow through because I've already experienced my future.

Some of my greatest moments of success or trajectory-changing decisions have come and been made from when I have felt absolutely petrified. In my experience, the scariest asks, reach-outs, offers, connections, and suggestions have all led to the biggest successes. My motto is, "Do it scared. Do it anyway." This has always served me. Playing small does not serve the world in any way. The world needs you to shine bright to give those around you permission to do the same. One of the most beautiful elements of the human experience is the fact that we are all completely unique and all have something special to offer the world. Your dreams matter because you are the only one who can do it the way that you can.

When I was about three or four years old, my family had a tradition of going out to dinner at the local Italian restaurant in Suffolk Park on Sundays. Conveniently, I would be wearing my most adorable dress because we would be passing there on our way back from our local congregation meeting in Lennox Head. They always had live music. At this restaurant they always had live music, there was a low stage where a guitarist would play solo sets. My parents loved hearing him play, but I loved it even more because I wanted to be a part of it. He made me feel like I could do it too.

With all the wisdom of a three-year-old, I started taking a little toy guitar with me each week to play along with him. I felt no shame whatsoever. The man would be seated center stage and I would sit at the front on a large step, my feet barely reaching the ground. I honestly believed I was a part of the band. There was a stage and there were people watching, so I was all-in! My mother says, to this day, that I was born a performer. I would continue the show even after the guitarist had left by performing dance solos for the whole restaurant. Can you imagine it?

When in your adult life, have you felt this level of freedom running through your veins? Even from a young age, I have always given myself radical permission to believe in myself to do what I love.

You deserve to see yourself in this way. The world deserves to see you shine. Today I want you to make the decision to adopt that new lease on life, where anything you want is possible. Allow yourself to fall in love with whatever your unique desire is for your reality and experience it fully. Let yourself become familiar with the specific inexpressible feelings your dream gives you, that feeling only you can know. Once you are familiar with the core essence of your goal, I want you to couple that with absolute belief, faith, and trust. If you truly know that you've had your dream for a reason, then the immediate next step is to tell yourself that it is meant to be and that you are absolutely going to achieve it. As hippie-dippie as this sounds (I know, optimism and idealism are not exactly *en vogue*) trust me, it works. After all, you are braver, stronger, smarter, more beautiful, more capable and more powerful than anything and anyone on planet Earth. There is no one like you! Being you is your power and believing in yourself is your birthright. It is time to claim them both now.

I want you to believe in yourself enough to know you're worthy and deserving of living that highest, truest, grandest vision you hold for yourself—the vision that holds everything you desire.

You can have it all.

I dare you to believe you can, because if I can, you can.

My Radical Permission Slip to Believe in Me!

Today on the __ of __, I give myself radical permission to go all-in, to expand, to grow, and to flourish so that I can have more impact in this world and more abundance in every area of my life. I am strong, deserving, and wholeheartedly worthy of my deepest desires. I give myself the official permission to curate the highest, truest, grandest vision I hold for myself. Today, I draw the line in the sand and go to the next level in all areas of my life. I give myself permission to achieve my desires.

I give myself permission to achieve the following desires:

In order to be free, I have to be me.
I declare to release these limits.
I believe in Me.

Date:_____ Signed:_____

I've decided that I will be shine as bright as I desire while being my unapologetic authentic self from this point forward!

3

WHERE THE WORLD
IS YOUR STAGE

In the play *As You Like It*, Shakespeare wrote:

> "All the world's a stage, and all the men and women merely players. They have their exits and their entrances, and one man in his time plays many parts…" (2.7.142-45)

No truer could this be when applied to the principle of believing in yourself and what's possible for you. The more we realize we are all players on the same stage (and let's be honest, we all have played many parts in life), it becomes increasingly more obvious that you need to believe in order to proceed with confidence, faith, deep courage, and unwavering belief.

In other words, if life is a game that we all are playing, then the only way to win at this game is by choosing to get off the bench and take center court. I want you to say to yourself, "I am committed to playing full-out." I often ask myself the following thought-provoking and decision-altering question:

> *Is what I am about to do, say, or think putting me on the success curve or the failure curve?*

Growing up, I loved track and field. If it had anything to do with running or jumping, I was all-in (due to my ballerina arms, throwing sports were never my thing. Why do people even enjoy throwing heavy objects anyway?). Somewhere between loving athletics, and adoring my P.E. teachers, Mrs. Buchanan (who even to this day is always there for me, helping and always going above and beyond to help me grow and succeed) Mr. Gal, Kelly C, Pricey, and Wilso, I was inspired by them all to become a P.E. teacher myself. They always had a vested interest in me. They have taught me to always go the extra mile to help and be present to invest in others. I love the saying by Zig Ziglar, "There are no traffic jams on the extra mile." These teachers, my role models, played in that lane.

When I finally achieved that goal, I had the opportunity to work full-time alongside these very teachers. My desk was nestled between theirs, in the staff room that I had once loved to visit so much. But now I had a place there. I'd done it. My beloved teachers had become my colleagues. The mentorship I received and the positive examples I saw are what have made me the teacher I am today. I wanted to be like them when I grew up, so much so that I made it a reality. Getting paid to go to track and field meets? I couldn't think of anything better!

In my senior year of high school– that's year 10 for all my Aussies–I attended a college fair that was showcasing different degree programs. During the question-and-answer session, the speaker asked for a show of hands to see who knew what they wanted to do in the future. I raised my hand. I didn't know the name of my desired career at the time, but in raising my hand, I knew I was saying yes to doing what I loved. In my mind, that was being involved with sports forever. However, I was never going to settle for a job I didn't love. Little did I know I would develop into an entrepreneur. The important thing is that I knew my dream was important, and so is yours.

Even though we know our dreams are achievable, sometimes we tend to find hundreds of reasons why they might be better off saved for later.

Believe me, I get it. It happens to us all.

A good way to remember the success or failure curve is to think of yourself as a professional athlete. You are the gold-medalist of your own life because, let's face it, believing in yourself is like going to the courage and resilience Olympics. Success comes down to being a part of the "No-Excuses World Championships." It's the call towards the next level of You in all departments, the call to become your best. You deserve to be on that stage, that court, that field, that podium. So, if that is your role, you have to ask yourself, would an Olympian be worthy of the gold medal if their actions, thoughts, and decisions leading up to the Olympics were things that put them on the failure curve? Obviously not, but the fact still remains that attaining success will require a level of personal sacrifice, focus, and commitment. Ask yourself, what are you willing to give up in order to win? Excessive scrolling through your phone? Negativity? Excuses? Damaging habits? Truly ask yourself, "Is what I am doing right now in my life, on my own stage, putting me closer or further away from attaining the gold medal of my own life?"

Like I said, once you've given yourself radical permission to wholeheartedly chase after your goal, the next step is making a conscious effort to take aligned action and move toward your destination with no excuses. I know this may sound scary, but allow me to share something extremely liberating with you:

"Ready" is not a feeling. It's a decision.

A common temptation you may encounter is the desire to wait until things "feel right," or until you "feel ready." This, my friend, is the ultimate trap. It is comforting to know is that this is just your subconscious mind attempting to protect you by making sure you play smaller and stay lesser than you actually are. It's all a subconscious effort to keep you safe by staying in your comfort zone.

The bottom line is, "I don't feel ready" is simply fear.

It may seem uncertain and scary to you but let me tell you what is certain: decades will go by without any change if you give in to your fears.

Imagine you're preparing for the hundred-meter sprint. Your spikes are on, you've trained, and you are as ready as you'll ever be. When you hear, "on your mark," you know there's no going back, as much as you feel like exiting stage left. "Set," and "go" are only seconds apart, and when you hear these words, you know there is only one thing to do: run as fast as possible toward the finish line.

How does this relate to your life? Just like an Olympic sprinter, this is your signal to move. Once you decide to start running, there's no walking off the track. Set your feet on the blocks and get ready because, if you don't, decades—maybe even your whole life—will pass you by. Naysayers will cost you your goals and you won't ever cross the finish line of your dreams. How many times have you asked for a sign, and then once you've gotten it, ask for an even bigger sign? How many times have you put your dreams on the shelf, just to be another gear in a much larger machine? As Courtney C. Stevens famously said, "If nothing changes, nothing changes."

If there is something of which I am fully persuaded, it is that we can't shine unless we are working on purpose, in alignment, and in flow towards what we want–not what others want. Progress is happiness and growth; the life force of all fulfillment. To put it simply, the "flow state" is the feeling of bliss associated with your work or what you're doing. I'm sure you've felt it before when doing something that you love. It's that feeling where you know you could continue to do something forever. Latching onto that mental state is going to be the real key to success in whatever it is you are trying to do. It enables you to push through and achieve the work you want, instead of putting it off until later.

Langston Hughes began his famous poem with the titular line, "What happens to a dream deferred?" and while he offered several potential answers, I can honestly tell you that nothing happens when you put off your dreams, and nothing will happen until you make a conscious choice to walk the path in full; wholeheartedly and unapologetically with full self-permission to go for it. That's the all-in commitment.

As a self-check to make sure I am staying on the success curve, I always like to ask myself these five questions:

1. Is what I'm about to do, say, or think, taking me closer to my goal, or further away?

2. Is what I am about to do putting me on the success curve, or the failure curve?

3. Does what I'm about to do align with my values and Future Self's essence and vision I have?

4. How would this situation expand me, the people in my life, and my future impact?

5. Is this giving me a full-body "Yes!" feeling?

I cannot stress how absolutely crucial these questions are in these moments of hesitation. Memorize them. Internalize them. Screenshot them. Repeat them to yourself at every turn. Write them on you if you need to, as long as you remember to filter your future decisions through this lens. If your answer to the last question is "Yes," then proceed. All steps towards your goal, no matter how small they are, are all drops of water that make an ocean. However, if your answer is "no," ask yourself if you are willing to make the necessary adjustments. Unless you can answer with a full-bodied, every-fiber-of-your-being "Absolutely. Yes!" then you won't be able to achieve your goal fully. But remember, "No." is also a full sentence and is something you will need to add to your vocabulary and use whenever necessary. If something is not taking you towards your goal, you will need to learn to say "no" to whatever it is. Only you can know specifically what you need to say "no" to, and only you can make the choice to do something different.

The choice to believe in yourself is one that is deeply personal and can only come from you. You are the only one with the power to make that decision. The fact of the matter is you don't need your friends and family to believe in you before you can do it yourself. Believing comes from within and reflects back to you. In my experience, I have found that all my biggest successes have come after I realized that everything I needed was already within me. As soon as I owned my innate power and went all in, I achieved success with ease, peace, and power. That is the difference between looking outside and looking within.

Your next task is to find the qualities you desire for yourself in other people. This is so that you can then breathe love and life into them, while also giving the same back to yourself. It's a powerful circle. So, when you see things in others that you admire, be rest assured that those attributes are already within you too. You wouldn't have noticed those qualities if you didn't already have them within you. The inverse is also the case. When you see something in yourself that you love, you will notice it in others around you and inspire change and self-acceptance with your influence. This is your chance not just to give yourself radical permission to follow your dreams, but also to provide the opportunity for others to make the same decision. Believing in others can truly change lives. Self-belief does not equate to self-absorption or self-centeredness, as one of the primary (and best) side effects is that believing in yourself is contagious. Once you can demonstrate this to others, they will want to try it for themselves.

I urge you to remind yourself that your success does not come from, nor is it based on, a feeling. It is based upon daily, active decisions. Deciding that you are worthy and have all the power within you to achieve anything is something you can do right now. Once you've mastered that, you'll be able to master anything that life brings.

You just have to choose to win.

Challenge 3

"Success Curve vs. Failure Curve"

Questions to keep you on the success curve:

- Is what I'm about to do, say, or think, taking me closer to my goal, or further away?

- Is what I am about to do putting me on the success curve, or the failure curve?

- Does what I'm about to do align with my values and Future Self's essence?

- How would this situation expand me, the people in my life, and my future impact?

- Is this giving me a full-body "Yes!" feeling?

- What am I going to replace these things with that will aid in my success?

The choice to believe in yourself is one that is deeply personal and can only come from you. Believing in yourself is a CHOICE!

4

KNOW WHAT YOU WANT

If I asked you, "what do you want?", how fast do you think you could give me an answer? Would you hesitate and ponder on it for a while, maybe giving a reserved answer after some serious consideration? Would you say what you think would make others around you happy? Or, would you immediately grab a laptop and projector to present a detailed PowerPoint on everything you have ever wanted since the age of six?

No matter which camp you fall into, at the end of the day, you would still be able to give some form of an answer. This is because everyone, if they are truly honest with themselves, knows exactly what they want, whether it's on a conscious or subconscious level. Quite often, our thoughts will tend to turn towards our desires whether we are consciously aware or not. The problem is, we can sometimes find it hard to identify clearly what that desire is beyond the abstract. Or even worse, we can sometimes be our own barrier to achieving our goals when we do not make a choice to actively go after what we want. This is why, as we continue on our journey of self-belief, knowing what you want and identifying it clearly is absolutely vital. Deciding what you truly want is a powerful feeling.

Out of every goal I have ever had, one stands out as the most. When I was 27, I joined a network marketing company and was immediately struck with the desire to reach the top level of the company. When I saw the top leaders in the company taking their annual holiday in Maui and being recognized on social media, I knew I wanted to do it too.

When I first joined the company, I was encouraged to go to the next network marketing conference on the calendar.

"Sure," I said, not even knowing where the next conference would be. As it turned out, it was in Las Vegas, so I booked my ticket straight away. I had no idea what to expect or what it would even be about, but I went anyway. I didn't know a single person at the event. I was a one-woman team in an arena of 25,000.

I found myself in awe of everything I was seeing. I had never seen dresses like the ones the ladies were wearing, or awards presentations like the ones the conference had. I remember thinking, "Is this real life, or did I take a wrong turn and end up at a pageant?"

One of the speakers at the conference made a lasting impression on me. She stood confidently before the audience in a stunning yellow jacket emphasizing that we could all rise to the same heights that she had. She told us we could do it too. She said that this was our opportunity to go for it. I thought to myself,

"Heck, if these women can do it, why not me? I'm no different. I'm going to do this."

As you already know, I love a good stage, so it goes without saying that I was one hundred percent in (sadly, this was not a guitar-friendly stage, but I digress). I remember when I spoke to my mum and brother later that day I told them,

"Just you watch, I'm going to be one of the biggest names in this company one day. They will know who I am. I'm going to return a year from now and walk that stage as a top member of the company." Judging by my mum's reply of,

"Oh darling," I could tell she was thinking that I was living in a fantasy land. But I went for it anyway and used the conference as fuel. I set my focus on my goal, stuck to my word, and did exactly what I set out to do. I reached the top of the company in nine months. One year after my solo conference experience, I returned with a team. I had gone from being a nobody in the industry sitting alone in the audience, to seeing my name in lights and walking the main stage six times—all in a custom dream gown from New York. The following year, I returned with thirteen other leaders and between us, we collected twenty-nine top awards.

Let me tell you, it was *wild*.

The greatest lesson I learned from this experience is that I only needed to see one person doing what I wanted to do in order to know that I could do it too. In doing so, I was able to see the ripple effect that accomplishing my dream caused. My team was inspired, and as a result, spread the same inspiration and drive to hundreds of others. You can create the same ripple effect in your life, but it starts with knowing what you want and going after it.

Our desires and goals, though they are as varied and unique as we are ourselves, tend to fall into three main subsets: health, wealth, and relationships. So much of our daily lives revolve around, or are directly influenced by these three things. Who at some point in their lives hasn't wanted to feel fitter and healthier, or had a desire to increase their income, fall in love, or deepen their connections with those around them?

If we break these aspects down further, the ideas of health, wealth, and relationships can be expanded into seven categories that impact our daily lives in various ways. When we want things, they will almost certainly fall into one of seven categories known as the "Seven Areas of Life."

Every new year, I hold a global call for my audience to spend the afternoon reflecting on the past year in all seven areas of life and gathering the lessons from it all. We work with intentionality and dissect each of the seven areas to make a rock-solid game plan for the upcoming year.

The first category is Relationships. Relationships are what tie each and every one of us together. If you think back carefully on your life up to today, you might realize that you have been defined by the series of connections you have made over time. Our quality of life is represented by the quality of our connections and community. That being the case, it's no wonder that we spend so much time fixating on our relationships. Our connections with others aren't just mere social interactions. They can actually have a massive impact on our longevity and quality of life. They also can define other granular aspects of our lives, down to our decisions and our moods. It is vital that you take extra special care in your relationships, as they are a big part of the rudder that guides your life.

The second is related to Emotional Strength. Being emotionally strong is all about approaching adversity in a vulnerable, honest way, making certain to learn from mistakes and prioritize a healthy outlook. Think of emotional strength almost as a suit of armor that protects you in your daily life. An emotionally strong person knows how to respond to roadblocks and how to bounce back from mistakes. Not everyone is able to do this. Maybe you've encountered people in your life or work that fall into this category. Maybe you've even had times where you did not feel emotionally strong yourself. When you encounter a problem, how much effort and intensity do you give it? Perspective is everything and our mindset is truly the greatest of all our assets.

The third category is Leadership, best defined as our ability to influence others towards a common goal. It is one of the most vital aspects of how we interact with the world. Whether you find yourself in the position of leading or being led, the vast majority of our interactions in life involve leadership in some way. Very often we picture ourselves as a leader in hypothetical situations. This is because at a core level, everyone has something that they believe in enough to want to bring others on board.

The fourth is related to your Fitness and Health. This isn't just limited to physical athleticism or dieting for the sake of it. An active, healthy lifestyle also promotes a strong and balanced mind. Our mental health is just as important as our physical fitness. When those two aspects are combined and prioritized, it can lead to a much happier and more positive outlook. Health is wealth, after all.

The fifth is Finance and Career. This aspect dominates so many of our wants because money is directly tied to every single area of our lives. Where is it going to come from? How long will it last? These are questions that are frequently asked when this fifth category is not being met.

The sixth category, Spirituality, is one of the most important. Faith in all forms is essentially how we react or respond to a revelation of something. Humanity has been searching for the answers to life's big questions since the dawn of time and will continue to do so until that time has run out. Spirituality is one of the many ways we as people seek to assign meaning and purpose to what can often seem like uncertainty. We have all at one point or another looked at our lives and asked, "What on Earth is going on?" Having a system of belief that allows you to see and know your purpose in all things can be a major comforting factor in our lives.

At five years old I was taught to memorize Psalm 83:18, "May people know that You, whose name is Jehovah, You alone are the most high over all the earth." This scripture has since become a favorite of mine. It had such an impact on me as a little girl that to this day I recite it often in my mind. I have always believed in God and have an appreciation for creation and all the things around me that prove to me over and over, day by day, that He exists. Ask yourself, what do you believe in? What's your personal spirituality?

Last, but certainly not least in importance, is our Contribution and Purpose in life. This is without a doubt the biggest category by way of scale. The very essence of all existence can basically be boiled down to the question of, "why am I here and what for?" In the same way that each person on Earth is unique in their own way, so too are our individual purposes. Everyone's capacity for contribution to the world is multi-faceted and varied, but the secret is that it is entirely up to you. Only you can be fully aware of the gifts, talents, and contributions that you want to bring forward into the world, and only you can put them into action.

As you think on these seven areas, challenge yourself to focus on those specific aspects that you would like to see yourself grow in. As daunting as self-examination may sometimes feel, remind yourself of this: no one that did the work didn't make it. Knowing specifically what you want is one of the most important steps to believing in yourself.

I genuinely believe anything is possible if you know what you want and work at it. Remember everything you want is on the other side of believing. So know exactly what you want in each category and BELIEVE!

"WHAT I DESIRE AND DEEPLY WANT"

- I believe that I am worthy and deserving of achieving the things I want for myself.

- My top 3 "wants" are:

- My #1 focus desire is:

7 AREAS OF LIFE:

1. Spiritual Awareness

2. Emotional Strength

3. Leadership/Your Career

4. Relationships

5. Health and Fitness

6. Financial Growth

7. Purpose & Contribution

If you can see it, imagine it, believe it and feel it. Then it was made for you.

"I CREATE my reality!"

5

DECIDE YOU ARE WORTHY

If there is something I know for certain, it is that the greatest gift you can give someone is to believe in them. I have always felt that believing in others aids them to feel deserving and worthy of their truth. This is why I believe that the most unconditionally loving thing we can do for someone is to wholeheartedly believe in them. Belief, especially when expressed towards others, has the ability to heal, move and transform in profound ways.

I took some time in Paris to celebrate my 20th anniversary as a mentor, coach and educator. It was a special moment. My brother and I had previously met up with one of my first-ever students, Simone, in Berlin a few weeks earlier where she did a photo shoot for me (so talented, that girl!). We did the math and realized that it had indeed been two decades since I taught her, and six other students, piano and dance lessons. As the saying goes, "When you do what you love, you never have to work a day in your life," and I have spent my entire career doing what I love.

Growing up in Byron Bay, Australia was an absolute DREAM! I mean if anyone has been there, I know you will agree. It's one of those little Aussie towns that is known around the globe. Everywhere I travel people know that name. I feel I can attribute the bright Australian sun and outdoor lifestyle to my Little Miss Sunshine personality. I have always had a bubbly, positive demeanor and when people ask why is your energy so happy and bright, I usually say I don't know what you even mean. However, when I think about it, I do know. It was embedded in me from a young age; a love of fun in the sun, outside playing and exploring. Life was FUN! I guess I just have a love for people and community, and that makes me happy and feel joy from within. I take that small town, start-local-go-global attitude with me all over the world. I never forget where I have come from and where I started. That down to earth Aussie, the hard-working, people-loving vibe is my trademark because that's just me in my natural state. Unapologetically, authentically me. Now from that little town I now create opportunities for people all over the world. Oh, and the Aussie accent does wonders overseas by the way!

From a child, we got to live five minutes from my school, the local dance school, the town center and the beach. We walked or rode our bikes everywhere. It was truly beachside living. My dad, was and is still the local painter that everyone loves. Our best friends lived next door, my Byron bestie Michelle Riordan and her beautiful family. Later in that same house, Georgia Madai and her lovely mum moved in. To this day Georgia is like the younger sister I never had and Michelle is like the older sister, I never had. As well as my gorgeous friend Carmen (Dubadee, she knows) who was my first best buddy and a plethora of lovely friends that I could all name through all schooling times, all such special friends. I still think of you all so often. I love you all and the chapters of life we all shared.

At age sixteen, the seed of teaching was planted. I embarked on my teaching journey in a few ways. I began teaching piano students from my home in "The Old Barn." My dad built a gorgeous wooden barn on our home property next to our house. It was for parties, sleepovers, accommodation, piano playing, and all the fun possibilities. It's a House family tradition to build a barn on your home property. There's many a barn built all over by my grandpa, uncle, and father. Next, I began tutoring younger students after school in their curricular studies, helping them with homework and assignments. That same year, I started my true love, assistant teaching at the local dance studio, Byron School of Dance, alongside the most renowned teacher from the area—the amazing and powerful Val Steward. My first Tap dancing class started at three years old because mum and I heard the tapping coming from the hall next door to the preschool. That hot summers afternoon, we listened to the tapping and went in to have a look, and I began that day, in that very lesson, and the rest is history. That class injected a love of all things dance and performance ever since, and now I have been dancing for over three decades. The memories of all the dance concerts, recitals, eisteddfod's, and class after class are to this day a highlight of my life. It was Val's overall training and the artistic brilliance of Deb Buen-Hortz and Sharnie Wilson, who made up the dancer, teacher, and a lot of the choreographer and artist I am today. They say dance stays with you a lifetime, and thanks to these three women, I have had a love of dance and performing arts that is so deep it will last a lifetime. It will never leave. Thank you beyond words for generously passing your skills on! It was from here my love of teaching grew and grew.

When I was eighteen, I took over the local dance studio and thereafter bought the business. The same day I made the purchase I graduated year 12 at Byron Bay High School, class of 2003! Six weeks later I began my Bachelor of Human Movement Science and Bachelor of Education at South Cross University. Over the next ten years, I taught twenty-five classes and countless private lessons, six days a week.

By age twenty-two, I began my dream job of teaching high school P.E., all while owning and operating my dance school, House of Dance. Following my graduation from undergrad, I taught for another six years. I was dubbed "Miss House" at the high school and "Miss Cassandra" at my dance school. To say I loved what I did is an understatement!

My love of teaching later led me to pursue my Masters in Education, as I still hoped to become a school principal one day. In addition to my degree, I opened a second dance studio. I also purchased and renovated a hair and beauty salon on the main street of Byron Bay. To cap it all off, I also opened two traditional dancewear stores with my own line.

At twenty-seven, I entered the world of network marketing through the health and wellness industry. I had the opportunity to teach, train, and coach thousands of men and women across six countries. At the same time, I began my PhD in Visualization for Sporting Performance, studying the relationship between visualization, execution, and performance.

At twenty-nine, with seven years of university, twelve Australian Teachers of Dancing diplomas, three degrees, ten years of business experience, five traditional businesses, and a network marketing business at the top level of leadership in the company, I sold all but my network marketing business, took leave without pay from school, and moved to New York City. I had the time of my life living in Brooklyn Heights.

After some time, I found myself wanting to return to Australia and resume my mission to become the principal of my own school. My desire was to teach my own future-focused curriculum centered around things like mindset, entrepreneurship, online business, leadership, and belief. I returned to teaching at the local high school and loved it just as much as I had before. Teaching is what made (and still makes) my heart feel alive.

It was at this time, however, that I was involved in a horrible car crash. While waiting at a red light, a truck towing a fully-loaded double trailer rear-ended me at 60 km. per hour. I suffered a back injury and whiplash, and as a result, was not able to return to school. I lost my contract and eventually, unable to recover in time, lost my right to return from leave at the school.

I was devastated.

I had been ready to take the education world by storm, but after seven years of study and a massive vision, everything ended in a flash. I learned, however, that sometimes things happen for reasons outside of our knowledge, or control. Had it not been for the accident, I might not have had the opportunity to take my love of education online. What began as a setback has now provided me with the opportunity to impact people around the globe. Over the years, I have used the skills I've learned to mentor many students to have businesses of their own. I am so proud of them all. It's a privilege to watch. Despite it feeling like an immediate roadblock (no pun intended), being in such a life-altering situation was a redirection for me that I am still coming to understand the blessing of–if a car crash can even be called a blessing. But each day its significance has become clearer. I am blessed to see how things are always working out in my favor. That is a belief I will always hold true. Because of my love for what I do, I have not missed a day of coaching, teaching, and mentoring for twenty years straight, and it's something I'm truly proud of. Being able to see people's lives transformed by your work is the greatest blessing.

As I look back at the last two decades, I may have been in different industries and environments, but a love for people and an insane desire to help others has been my consistent objective.

The reason I have told you these stories is to challenge you to reflect and ask yourself whether you are spending each day doing what you love no matter what. If you could do anything tomorrow and get paid to do it, what would it be? If everything was taken care of and you had the time and financial means to look after yourself and your family, what would you do? Is that what you get to do each day? If not, then why? Don't let your past experiences and obstacles hold you back from living a life that you love.

I am so passionate about helping people monetize their genius and get to do what they love daily–this is my next twenty-year mission. I train coaches in my Coach the Coach program. I create courses for people who want to share their ideas to the world and turn them into thriving six & seven-figure businesses. I help inventors and start-ups go through the motions of taking their products to market, as well as helping people write, publish, and promote their own books. I empower entrepreneurs in my collective, inner circle, to help them create their dream lives, all while partnering with many legends of the industry, coaching teams, and corporate executives all over the world.

I love showing people how to build their own empire instead of building someone else's. You get two choices in life: build someone else's empire or build your own.

You get to choose that daily.

I have always been a big believer that education is the greatest and most impactful piece of art you can give someone because it lasts forever. There is power in education. I use what I know to help people learn how to make their dreams become a reality, and not only that, be rewarded lucratively for it.

When I reflect on my work, the people-focused aspects have proven to be one of the most rewarding facets of my life. To help, teach, and empower others is a part of how I am able to show love to others. It is something that I constantly encourage those I meet to incorporate into their lives. You don't even have to be a teacher to do it, and a good way to start is through supporting family or friends in their individual dreams, businesses and endeavors.

However, there is one more important person to whom you should show love, through belief, and that person is yourself. Loving yourself and always having your own back is key. Without challenges, we can neither change nor grow. "It is what it is" is one of my favorite sayings. With this mindset you can believe in yourself through any adversity. Self-belief is what got me through the car crash I was in, a house robbery that happened on my honeymoon, dissolved friendships, death of loved ones, massive highs followed by shattering lows, low seasons that last a while longer than a season, judgment, betrayal, pain, false accusations, regret and hurt. We all face difficulties and challenges in our lives, and I am no different. No matter where you have come from, no matter what you have gone through, please know that you can overcome it all when you believe in yourself and decide that you are worthy. Often, we have everyone else's back, but it's important to remember that the first oxygen mask we need to put on is our own. I told you my stories, lessons, and memoirs for one reason only. Just know we all go through things, and no matter how big or small they are to us individually, you can make it through anything. You are stronger than you think.

Believe bigger. Trust Stronger. Faith it all the way through. We are in this together.

Believe! Because if I can, you can too.

CHALLENGE 5

TAKE INVENTORY!

Are you truly doing what you LOVE?

If you could do anything tomorrow and get paid to do it, what would you do? (This may take time to come up for you) So be patient and honor yourself where you're at and let it come.

Just think if you had endless funds and no need to trade time for money or work just to pay the bills what would you CHOOSE to do with your hours, days, weeks, months, and years?

The greatest gift you can give someone is to BELIEVE in them!

6

YOU HOLD THE KEY TO
YOUR WORTHINESS

D o you ever feel scared and totally unworthy of that next jump? You may have read my story and thought, *how will I ever take the leap and do what I love daily?* Maybe you already love what you do but you want to feel more fulfilled in it. It all comes down to the level of worthiness you hold for yourself. Your standards are defined by the things you settle for. For example, there is something I do to make everything make sense for me:

I keep a collection of childhood photos saved on my phone. My camera roll is an absolute menagerie of old memories. One album is completely populated with pictures of "Little Cass." I even have a screen saver of them all collaged. Written over them are encouraging messages to her, like:

I believe in you.

I support you.

You're safe, protected, loved, and looked after.

You deserve this dream.

We're strong adults now. We are safe.

Everything is going to be okay. We've got this.

These messages are so important to me. It is a constant reminder to be kind to myself (every Self I have ever been, past and present) that I am worthy of the dreams that Little Cass had, and that no one in the world can stop them.

I find that, even if we know what we want, a challenge we can often face is the feeling of not being deserving of those desires. This is almost always because we hold, as Thais Sky originally called them, "worthiness wounds," or trauma sores. Worthiness wounds are something that we have all experienced, though the sources from which they arise are many and varied. It may be because you were told that you were not good enough or that you were inadequate in some way as a child; that a busy parent once forgot to pick you up from school, or you were not listened to fully when you needed it most. It might be that none of these things were done on purpose, as many of these early traumas can just be attributed to our perspective as children. It may be a memory you had as a child that your other siblings don't share because of your different experiences. Whatever your experiences, they are all valid and accepted. Sometimes these wounds are scars we still hold to this day, ones that often appear decades later.

You may see it show up as fear of abandonment, rejection, or a tendency to procrastinate. They may come from fears of all sorts or some other way in which emotional needs were not being met. Worthiness wounds almost always stem from trauma, and they can sometimes feel like insurmountable obstacles. As we go throughout our lives, like any injury, worthiness wounds will continue to fester and reopen if they are not healed. We might see evidence of them through the onset of imposter syndrome or self-deprecation. They heavily impact our ability to be confident in our dreams and to go after them as we should.

The worst thing that can be done with a worthiness wound is to ignore it, or to put an emotional band-aid over it. The old adage, "out of sight, out of mind," does not in any way apply to worthiness wounds. The more often we experience them, the more we are shackled by them, and as a result we can become progressively more armored. It's a natural response for the ego to step in and act as a shield in traumatic or difficult situations, but ultimately what we might subconsciously think is self-protection may be the very thing holding us back. The only way to overcome a worthiness wound is to address it. Identifying the hurt, acknowledging it, giving ourselves permission to feel it and developing the courage to push forward in spite of it is the only way to nurture it and ultimately bring about healing.

This is not to say that this process is necessarily easy, as we all have different life experiences, wounds, and triggers that can often make facing up to our trauma difficult. You might find yourself focusing excessively on seemingly innocuous comments that set off thought spirals of inadequacy or self-doubt. Often this is because our overly protective ego is constantly searching for confirmation bias to prove itself right. Too much of this, and we can start to see our worthiness wounds in everything.

When I am faced with these feelings, trust me, I get them too, I'm consciously reminded of my younger self, and the fact that her dreams and aspirations still matter. I can say to myself, *"This isn't just a trigger. It's the worthiness wound being poked at."* So, when I bring Little Cass in and nurture her, the feelings subside almost instantly.

The most liberating piece of advice that I could give myself or anyone else is that you are a grown adult with the world at your feet. You can be, do, have, and achieve anything. The younger version of you, with their heart so full of dreams, had those goals for a reason. To this day, even as this book is being written, my lock screen on my phone has a letter to Little Cass.

It reads like this:

I see you, Little Cass. I have your back. We're safe now. I'm not leaving you. I love you. I've got you. Everything is always working out for us. You are so deserving and worthy of our dreams together. Let's do this! Let's paint the town red!

I love you little Cass, we are safe now. I got you, I have your back. I'm not leaving you we are together now. We are deserving of all the things we dream of.

Everything is working out of us! I love you and I belive in you

The world is our oyster let's paint the town RED!

This is something I read often, and it is a vital reminder of what is most important to focus on. I hope you might do the same in writing to your 'little' self and give yourself the same reminders, because you were worthy then, and you are worthy now.

Get a photo of a little version of you at approximate age 4 to 7 years old and put them somewhere close, like on your phone like I do, or printed in a frame.

The message I want to speak to the little version of myself is:

Everything you want is on the other side of BELIEVING! You are worthy and deserving to have it ALL! BELIEVE IT!

7

LOOK FOR GREEN

Quite often I find myself doing something I call, "looking for green". What I mean by this is I am always on an active search for things that are in flow with my purpose–things that are going my way and point towards me being in alignment.

"Ahh, I manifested that! I'm so in alignment," I find myself saying throughout the day when things easily and freely fall into place.

Green is our signal to move forward.

Green means "Go!"

Green is alignment.

Human beings are energetic by nature. By energetic, I don't necessarily mean how you feel after your second cup of coffee in the morning, but that we are constantly receiving and transmitting intangible energy. Have you ever met someone or gone somewhere and were instantly struck with a conclusive feeling or opinion about the encounter–a feeling that can't really be explained? Some might call it "catching a vibe," but what you really felt was the person's energy. Our actions, intentions, and goals are all charged with it, and it is possible to operate at different energy frequencies, or vibrations, in our day-to-day life.

Most commonly there are seven different types of vibrations, it can best be described by Schneider's Energy Leadership Scale, or more specifically, the seven levels that we as leaders can operate on. These energy levels have always been a powerful directive for my growth as a leader and in building leaders. To quickly summarize them, here is a brief description of each level:

- LEVEL 1 "The Lose-Lose Situation" - This first level of emotion is the lowest vibration and is often associated with negative emotions such as insecurity, powerlessness, guilt, sadness, and doubt. It goes without saying that this is not a healthy vibration level. This is when you, in fear and anger, are expecting both yourself and the other person to lose. Leading from fear guarantees that there is no gain for either party.

- LEVEL 2 "I Win, You Lose" - The second level of vibration centers around scarcity and lack. It prioritizes taking advantage of others for personal gain and has its roots in vindictive and resentful behavior patterns. This can be seen often in low levels of leadership where one-upmanship and seeking success through pushing others down is the norm. This is where the leader wins at the loss of another team member. It is extremely low vibration and one fueled with jealousy and revenge.

- LEVEL 3 "We Both Win or We Don't Play" - This third level prioritizes cooperation, collaboration, fairness, and an even scale. This level can still be leading from blame, worry and doubt, but also can be associated with complacency or boredom. This is the minimum level of vibration that one needs to surpass before anything positive can even be experienced. This is the first level where manifestations begin. The lower vibrations in contrast will likely only attract things that are undesirable or unwanted. This level will attract mostly negativity with an occasional hint of positivity.

- LEVEL 4 "Everything is Working Out for Me" - This level is where I aim to set my daily thermostat at a minimum. It is a bold statement. It's something that I repeat to myself often, and I highly recommend that you start your day by doing the same. This can allow for a much more positive outlook centered on expectation, hopefulness, excitement, and anticipation of what is to come.

- LEVEL 5 "I Live a Blessed Life" - The fifth level is centered entirely on belief, trust, and faith. It is based on a confident knowing, not based on the abstract but in the appreciation of the moment. This level along with the previous fourth level are my personal favorites to operate in. It is possible to learn to live in levels 4 and 5 as a daily decision. Each day I begin with these two affirmations to remind myself that no matter what happens, I live a blessed life and that the way will continue to open. This mindset can be summarized in the following affirmation: *I have unconditional faith and trust that everything is working out for me, in my favor, and for the goodness of all, because The Universe has my back.*

- LEVEL 6 "It's All an Experience" - The sixth level of emotion is expressed through treating all occurrences as part of the experience of life. This is not to say that this is a level of passivity, but rather a state in which you are objectively viewing whatever happens to you as part of a larger, more nuanced story that is bigger than the individual moments themselves. It is

a level of non-attachment where we lead with opti-
mism, eagerness, and happiness.

- LEVEL 7 "I Am the Observer of the Observer" -
This final stage is almost akin to a bird's-eye-view
of your life. It is a more enlightened state in which
you can step back and observe your surroundings,
imagine their complexity, and make judgments based
on rational surveyance. *How do I feel at this moment?
How will I choose to react? Where could I have done
things differently today?* This level requires the highest
degree of self-awareness and is only experienced in
mere glimpses when we are truly present and aware.
It is a level of complete joy, freedom, enlightenment,
and passion.

Now that we've got that all covered, you might be asking
"But Cass, what does this have to do with looking for green?"
The answer is, well, everything.

If I asked you to identify all the things that were good
in your life, you'd likely be able to give me an answer. But
if I asked you to list all the things that are negative in your
life, would that list outstrip the good? Only you can answer
honestly, but if I could guide you, I would say to begin to
look at everything that comes your way through the lens of
the higher vibrations. To return to the metaphor of green
lights and red lights, think of the first three levels as your red
lights. These can be golden opportunities to do a self-check.
The higher vibrations, however, are your green lights. When
you are operating at that level, you are much more equipped
to make decisions and remain in a mindset that will take
you towards your goal. Those green lights are your blessings.
They are moments of full-body alignment where you are in
the right place at the right time. You only have to wait for it,
and when it finally comes, there's only one thing to do: take
it in and embrace it fully. It's not the things we have, but the

moments we remember. Embracing your incredible life, no matter what stage you're in, allows you to move from red to green. In life, you choose how you feel every day. You're behind the wheel, no one else.

Floor it.

I commit to keeping a miracles journal.

Today the miracles I experienced are:

I have seen lots of green today. This is when:

I have unconditional faith and trust that everything is working out for me, in my favor and for the goodness of all, The Universe has my back. Everything is working out for ME, I live a blessed life!

8

IDENTIFY THAT YOU'RE
DESERVING

Before we go any further, allow me to establish something right out of the gate: You are a total boss worthy and deserving of it all whether you know it or not. Sometimes when we have desires, our first instinct is to think, "Can I do that?" That instinct to automatically cancel ourselves out is an overworked reflex for some, but in reality, it's just forgetting all of the amazing things you've accomplished. Allow me to release you from the urge to heed that instinct. From here on out, we are banning "can I do that?" from your vocabulary.

There is no longer the need to ask because you absolutely can.

Do you realize what you're made of? Have you ever stopped to think that you are carefully created and designed with every hair on your head numbered and known? You are an absolute living work of art that has been chiseled like a beautiful sculpture, and yet you still question whether or not you are deserving? Today is the day I want you to realize how utterly beautiful, powerful and deserving you are, and then start living in it. No one other than yourself can be a greater ambassador for the wonder that you can, and will, create. Whether you realize it or not, you are the billboard of your life. You have to be proud of yourself and pitch You to the world, just like you'd sell anything else. Think you're not in sales? Think again, my friend. The fact of the matter is, you sell You every day of the week. We are all in sales *and then* we have other jobs. You are the face of your life, your business, and your family, and I want you to realize how phenomenal you truly are. There is something spectacular that you need to bring to the world and no one else is like you. No one else can give your gifts to the world except for you, and it is absolutely crucial that you realize it.

Whenever I struggle with believing in myself, I think of the things I've accomplished. I think of times in the past when I was unsure or felt unworthy, yet I still went for it anyway. I would tell myself, "Why not? Others have done it too." In retrospect, I wonder why I was ever worried. The capability was always there from the very beginning. Thinking back on my previous wins when I'm feeling low allows me to remind myself that I've had this all along. That's the real secret: the most important thing to do when identifying that you're deserving is to bring your many accomplishments to the forefront of your mind. You might be a super-mum who can expertly look after a gaggle of kids, take amazing care of a home, and make autobahn-speed school runs before rushing off to work an intricate job that routinely requires you to leap over tall buildings in a single bound. Maybe you're an amazing artist or creative talent who values imagination and innovation. Or you might even be a survivor who's been through it all and seen it all, and your perseverance is an accomplishment all on its own. No matter your story or what your day-to-day looks like, you deserve to give yourself the flowers. Take a moment to look back at the times when you have put your mind to something and saw it through. Think about where you've come from and who you are. This is your time to celebrate You and everything that you bring to the table every single day because they are not just a laundry list of accomplishments. They are tangible examples of the fact that you can, and do, make amazing things happen on the daily.

～∞∞～

So, let's do an exercise: You already know what you want, and you've given yourself radical permission to chase it. With that in mind, I want you to grab a pen and paper and write your biggest desire at the top of the page in bold letters. Draw a line down the middle and on the left side, write all the things that achieving your goal will bring you. Then on the right column, write out all the things that you bring to the table. What you'll find out is that there is going to be more on the right side. Because each success you've had in your own personal journey, the big and the small, were all steppingstones to your current location.

The realization that you actually bring a lot forward is going to be your biggest motivating factor in identifying that you are completely worthy and deserving. For instance, if your desire is to increase your income or to gain a much-deserved promotion in your work, that paycheck or new position will always be a reminder that you are on the right track. Use your successes as representations of all the lives that you have helped, and the milestones you have hit along the way.

If your desire is for an increased capacity for self-love, write that down. Write a list of things that you may not like, and then compare it with a list of things that you adore about yourself. You may even discover things you like about yourself that you may not have noticed. The fact of the matter is, you won't fully realize how incredible, powerful, and accomplished you are until you take that step back to look at your own story on paper. I want you to look at yourself like the piece of art that you absolutely are. While you're making your list, really hone in on those details that make you feel like the best version of yourself. Whatever they are, I want you to fall in love with You. Even if there are things about yourself that you don't like, keep in mind that they are all minor. The only thing you can do with them is to bless and release them. Love them anyway. If you resist them, they'll only get bigger.

The reticular activating system in our brains is trained to search for confirmation of what it wants to see, so turn them around. Nothing on Earth is completely perfect, and it is in imperfection that we can still find nuance, value, beauty, utility, and freedom. It all just comes down to how you perceive it. The truth is, if you change the way you look at things, the things you look at change. Ask yourself what kind of lens you use to look at life. Does it emphasize the negative or elevate the good? Take something like your phone, for example. The case may be faded, and the screen may be cracked (who hasn't watched in horror as their phone tumbled out of their hands and belly-flopped on solid concrete?) but that still doesn't change the fact that it's the tool you run your business with or use to hold precious memories and keep up with friends and family. Those imperfections are there, but the ability to achieve its designed purpose still remains.

The same is true with you.

You are already so equipped to achieve your dreams and are absolutely deserving of them, because everything you have ever needed to achieve your desires is precisely what it took to get you to where you are right now.

You are an astonishing work of art and you are deserving of it all.

Draw a line down the middle of a sheet of paper so there are two columns.

Left-hand side heading says: The Goal I Want

On the right-hand side: What I Bring to the Table

When you expect it, know it's done, and believe it to be true, that's when it will manifest! You will always get what you TRULY want, whether you like it or not. You will get what you expect EVERY time.

9

THE QUALITIES YOU POSSESS

You're seated at your computer, hands wringing over an online job application. Even though you've crossed your "t's" and dotted your "i's", you can't seem to stop double, triple, quadruple checking over things you've already read a hundred times. *What is it about this process that brings up so much angst?* You think to yourself, too nervous to consider the fact that you're sweating (like, literally sweating) and you've only just gotten past the phone number and address section. "Surely, I know that much," you say because it's not the personal info or even the work history rundown that has you apprehensive. The cursor hovers over two letters above the "next" button, two letters that are the reason behind the fact that your stomach has been audibly bubbling for the past five minutes: "CV."

What is it about a CV that tends to make so many of us want to run for the hills? How does one really sum up the entirety of our working lives in just two or three pages? Well, what if I told you that the CV is not something to be feared, but eagerly embraced.

"How on earth is that even possible?" you might ask, and the answer is this: it is a golden opportunity for you to do a self-audit and identify all the amazing qualities that you possess. Just like when we made a conscious effort to focus on the aspects of ourselves that we love, the same rules apply here. Consider all the skills that make you the person that you are today. What are those skills that you've spent your life honing? Is it a knack for numbers or savvy business thinking? Is it your team player attitude and your capability to influence others for good? Maybe it's your innovative spirit and ability to think outside of the box for some real 5D problem solving. Whatever those qualities are, own them. Just imagine what you could do if you actually went all-in and believed in yourself. We all have been blessed with unique qualities and talents and it is everyone's right to own and leverage them for themselves. You literally owe it to yourself to place trust in your qualities and attributes. They are all individual pieces of what makes you unique.

Challenge yourself and start to catalog these attributes that you are truly proud of—the things that make you feel most like yourself. When you really commit to doing the work and perform an honest self-audit, you'll be surprised just how many wonderful skills and qualities you identify within yourself. No one is a better spokesperson for what you can do than you, and it's your job to give yourself the best CV possible, both literally and figuratively speaking. But don't think of it just as something to use for a job or promotion. Think of your CV as a representation of you: your qualifications, your skills, and your abilities. The ultimate goal of all of this is to get to know just how powerful you are and to remind yourself what YOU bring to the table.

Something I like to do is take the Seven Areas of Life that we talked about earlier on and write down everything that I've accomplished in each of them already. This is just a simple method of taking stock of your own skills. What you'll find is that you'll be more confident in the future if you are able to look back over your accomplishments with pride. Next time you find yourself doing a self-audit, approach it with the confidence of someone successful in each of the areas of their life, knowing it will propel you further towards your goal.

You can always win. After all, you're you.

What I have already achieved in these areas of life:

- Spiritual Awareness
- Emotional Strength
- Leadership/Your Career
- Relationships
- Health and Fitness
- Financial Growth
- Purpose & Contribution

It is what it is, until you BELIEVE it to be different!

10

FEEL YOUR DESIRES INTO REALITY

I magine for a moment that you are standing on the edge of a riverbank. There's a beautiful crystal blue stream running ahead of you and on the far side, faintly above the rush of water, you can hear music. It's not just any music, mind you, it's your favorite song on full blast. You peer across, raising a hand to shield your eyes from the sun, and off in the distance, you can see your Future Self having the time of their life. They (or should I say, you?) are surrounded by everyone and everything you love. Your family and friends are gathered around you in what seems like a celebration. In fact, you know it's a celebration because your smile is the biggest and your laugh is the loudest. They're celebrating your greatest desire finally being achieved.

"Wow, that's some party," you think from your side of the river, altogether stunned by the sheer enormity of what you are feeling at that moment. Your Future Self looks content, happy, and satisfied. Their joy is one that you know is real, the kind of joy you can only get from having seen the journey through to the end, and you're watching the grand finale live and in person.

"There's no way they're going to play my song and I miss out on it," you think, and it is then and there that you decide you're going to cross the river even if it is the last thing you do.

You take stock of your options:

You look ahead at the space between you and the party (where they've cranked the music up louder now as if beckoning you onward) and you can see five huge river rocks peeking above the water. The first one is within jumping distance, so you steel yourself, hum a bar of that favorite song and leap out over the stream. You land on the rock with a satisfying *thud*. On the far bank, some of the party goers have started to take notice of you.

"You can do it!" you say to yourself.

"Don't you give up on me!" your Future Self shouts, raising a glass.

You know you can make it to the other side. The next river rock is slightly further, but you've already made it this far and there's no way you're going back to your former, tuneless side of the river. You make the next leap, and the next one, and the next, and the one after that. Each represents an essential move towards the next goal to make it over until your feet finally land firmly on the other side. The crowd erupts into deafening applause of sheer celebration as you arrive. You are welcomed by your Future Self.

"We were waiting for you to show up," they say, and you agree that this powerful, worthy, and deserving version of yourself was inside you all along.

—❦—

We all know what it's like to feel "FOMO", otherwise known as the Fear of Missing Out. This has to be one of the worst yet most motivating feelings. No one wants to be on the outside looking in. However, I tend to see things in another light. I rarely feel as if I am missing out. Instead, what I get is a profound surge of inspiration. I think, "If they can, I can." This is one of the secrets to my success. I have always believed in myself and what I want to achieve, knowing that it's done. There's nothing more frustrating than seeing where you want to be from a distance. It's from this feeling though, that we can all draw our motivation to cross the river. It's not just the party that spurs you onward or the distance between the river rocks, it's the feeling associated with getting there, and the satisfaction of having achieved it. Something you will need to constantly remind yourself of is that you are not chasing a thing, you're chasing the feeling attached to it. We never strive to accomplish something for what it is, we do so for the feeling associated with that accomplishment.

Picture how it felt to leap from rock to rock. Imagine each step as something that you need to do to move you closer to your dream. Through being intentional and memorizing the feelings that our dreams evoke within us; we can actually manifest them into our reality. We don't get what we want, we get how we feel. We get what we believe.

Something you may not have realized is that there is immense power in your vision. Becoming familiar with the sensory element of the vision you hold for your future; the way it makes you feel and the motivation it raises in you is a perfect opportunity to experience what it will be like to achieve your desire before it actually happens. When you know the feeling by heart it will be easier to recreate it for yourself until it is reality. Latching onto the excitement, anticipation, and sheer, giddy joy that your goal brings you during the journey itself is just as important as the feeling of accomplishment you will have at the end. Leaping from stone to stone, or working harder than ever on yourself, takes courage. The jump to each next step is a literal leap of faith. But it is the feeling of getting there, the feeling of knowing, as if it's already happened, that gets us to the next rock.

"RIVERBED MEDITATION"

Describe the feeling of celebrating your dreams into reality on the farthest side of the river. Bring it to life.

What were your key feelings associated with this celebration?

*The journey has to feel like
the destination feels...*

11

FROM FEAR TO LOVE

Over the past twenty years I've had the opportunity to teach and speak in front of thousands of people, and every time, no matter how charged up I am beforehand, I feel a small twinge of nervousness. It's not full-blown hyperventilating, faint-onstage-and-tumble-into-the-audience stage fright, but the jitters are definitely real. What I've learned however is a trick to make good use of those feelings by channeling that nervousness into excitement.

Imagine if you went to the pool and you saw someone put their goggles on backwards then take a swan dive into the deep end. I think we can both agree that would look pretty ridiculous, right?

Well, what if I told you that focusing on our feelings of anxiety and fear when chasing our goals is just about as helpful as wearing a pair of swim goggles backwards. In order to see the way forward, our lenses need to be pointed outwards, both metaphorically and literally speaking. Instead of solely devoting my attention to the fact that I may be nervous within the moment, I turn my vision towards looking out into the audience. I focus on serving, helping, and giving to other people, and the excitement associated with it. I tell myself, *I'm not scared, I'm excited! I'm excited for the opportunity to even speak to this audience and give to those that have so selflessly shown up to hear me.* By taking myself out of the equation, I have much more room to love and serve those around me. I approach each situation I encounter with gratitude—for my dreams and goals and the fact that I am able to impact so many lives through my work. What this continues to prove true in my life is that love is the secret antidote to any feeling that isn't aligned with your truest, highest vision that you've set for yourself.

When you feel that pang of nervousness and apprehension over what others might think of you or whether or not you actually have the ability to achieve what you want to, be reminded of the backwards goggles and turn your intention outwards. There's nothing wrong with feeling fear; it is a natural human emotion. When those feelings arise, the only thing to do is look at them and tell yourself, *I'm grateful for this opportunity. I'm excited to be here. I don't have to do this–I get to do this.*

I'm reminded of an occasion where I was asked to teach for an hour with only fifteen minutes' notice. I could have, at that moment, shrunk or shone. I chose to shine. Instead of being scared, I channeled my nervousness into excitement. I've also been in other situations where I've found myself slightly outside my comfort zone, and the first things out of my mouth were,

"Oh, my goodness, I'm so scared,"

and,

"Oh my goodness, I'm so excited!

The funny thing is that both of these reactions happened in the same breath. That's entirely because despite whatever I might have been feeling in that first instant, I could still see the gratitude in it. Something a lot of people don't know is that fear and excitement exist on the same vibrational level. When you are consciously aware of this, it's easy to transition from one to the other. Reminding yourself of why you are excited about your dream and expressing gratitude for the opportunities that have been placed before you are the quickest and most effective fear neutralizers.

There's one specific thing I focus on to shift my perspective in moments of stage fright. Instead of focusing on myself, I focus on the audience. I'm always impacted by the fact that people have taken the time out of their day to hear me speak. I may be the one on stage, but it isn't ultimately about me. It's about them. It's about you, the reader.

The first set of questions I often ask myself when faced with feelings of anxiety are:

- What more can I do for my audience?

- What more can I do for my team?

- What more can I do for my family?

- What more can I do for myself so I can love and serve more?

This is how I consciously change my perspective. Instead of focusing on my fears, I focus on the fact that I am here to serve.

The next time you find yourself apprehensive or afraid, just remind yourself of all the things that you're grateful for, the things you love about what you're doing. Ask yourself what you can do to help those around you, with the knowledge that it truly will change everything for you.

And remember the swimmer with the backwards goggles. You don't want to be that guy.

What am I fearful of? How can I rewrite these to become excited?

Fear 1:

Excited Statement:

Fear 2:

Excited Statement:

I am so GRATEFUL, I GET to do this! I am excited!

12

CHOOSE YOUR FEELINGS
TO LIVE BY

If you were to see my house or office, I can guarantee the
first thing you'd notice is the inordinate amount of post-it
notes plastered on every surface. On each, I've written
words like,

"Fun."

"Excited."

"Accomplished."

"Proud."

"Loved."

Of course, you, being a polite guest, would ignore the
enormous collection of multicolored page scraps wallpapered
to desks, mirrors, cabinets, and to be honest, most flat sur-
faces in general. Or maybe you'd ask me straight up what the
post-it thing is all about and I'd tell you that these are my
energetic values.

"What are energetic values, Cass?" you'd ask, and natu-
rally, that's where I would share a mind-blowing secret with
you: by leaving these messages around for me to constantly
read, I am creating every possible opportunity to live my life
based on those feelings. It's like the story of the river, right?
Each one of the five stones it took to get across can be seen

as one of those values. Once you can identify what your specific energetic values are, you can begin to engage with every aspect of your life based on those terms. The real trick here is that you get what you feel. You can think it, you can write it, or you can say it. It all plays a valid part in painting your future. You really start to attract what you want when you can feel it. This isn't always going to be easy, and it will definitely take you outside your comfort zone, but that's a sign that it's working. Your comfort zone is the direct opposite of life in line with your energetic values. When you're in that comfort zone, it's like standing on one side of the river and watching the party on the other side from a distance. You have to get to the other side by living out your values, daily.

My five personal energetic values are Fun, Excitement, Love, Accomplishment, and Pride. I make sure that I am spending every moment of each day living out these values to the fullest. I make decisions based on my energetic values and I continue to make sure that my biggest goals are all things that bring about those feelings. Do you know what the craziest thing about it is?

It works.

Whatever feelings are attached to your greatest goal, choose the top five and write them on post-it notes. List them on your screensaver. Then actually do things and say "yes" to things in your life that make you feel those feelings. Remember: the journey needs to feel like the destination feels.

I'm able to manually set my feelings every day, and so are you. It's like having a setting dial for good vibrations. The truth of the matter is, nobody can operate at one hundred percent if they're vibrating at zero. You need to search for good things, say "yes" to them, and go about your life doing what brings you all the feelings of your energetic values.

But that isn't quite enough just on its own. The last and most important thing to do after setting your feelings is to make sure you celebrate them. If you do or create something that makes you feel accomplished, celebrate it. The best part of all of this is that once you start living through your energetic values, it will begin to attract more of what you are looking for. Setting your feelings is pretty much the world's greatest lifehack. By consciously saying "yes" to the feelings connected to your ultimate desire, you basically turn yourself into a magnet for more of those feelings and experiences.

If the journey must feel like the destination feels, then why wouldn't you want to exist in those feelings every day?

And, while you're at it, cover your house in post-it notes.

"THE JOURNEY HAS TO FEEL LIKE THE DESTINATION FEELS."

What are your five key feelings?

Write each feeling on index cards or post-it notes and place them around your home.

When you get the chance, I hope you choose to DANCE!

13

GOAL SETTING

There are three people in a pool:
The first is wading in the shallow end, more concerned with their tan than the swimming, really. A slightly overcast sky will soon signal them to leave, beating a merry escape to wherever else is dry.

The second is a few feet away from the first, standing waist deep. Their expression reads, *you rotten little kids had better not get my hair wet or I'll turn this whole pool upside-down.* They probably will.

The third is many feet above our scene on the high dive, hair drenched, mascara running, giddy smile plastered across their face.

"Look out, world! I'm coming down!" they yell before leaping off the diving board and crashing, limbs splayed, into the water below. It is ungraceful. It is beautiful. It is, quite frankly, hilarious.

All three of these people were in the same pool, but which of them was really *in* the pool?

If there is one thing to be learned from our swimmers, it's that how you do anything is how you do everything. Are you someone who is content to doggy paddle around the shallow end, or are you someone who goes all out and dives straight in?

The key to all of this, to everything we've been talking about so far, is intentionality. Commitment gets you started. Consistency is what will take you to the finish line. Being intentional is the number one thing that leads to goal achievement. Period.

Having a game plan and sticking to it is one of the most important things you will need to be able to do as a leader. People want to follow those who know where they're going. Would you be particularly thrilled to fly on a plane with a pilot who had no idea where to go? I know I wouldn't. I'd feel safer with a parachute at 18,000 feet. Clear direction, combined with conscious intent, is how I get things done.

The most important thing in being intentional when achieving your desires is to give your goals a deadline. If you don't have a specific date or time that you intend to achieve what you want, odds are you'll end up putting it off indefinitely. But if you tell yourself, "I'm setting a deadline of XYZ-date," you'll be more likely to make a concerted effort to put the work in.

Personally, I like to write out my goals, set a date for each of them, and then stick them next to my bed so I can look at them every morning when I wake up, and at night when I go to sleep (here come the post-it notes again). There is something truly powerful about seeing your goals written down with a deadline attached. That deadline is the engine that is going to fuel your drive to see things through to the end.

Another reason why I love a good deadline is that it creates a sense of urgency. I believe that–when going after our goals–if we have all the time in the world, we *will take* all the time in the world. We've all had experiences where we have something major to prepare for yet have put it off right until the last second. But the truth is, most of what we need to do doesn't take that long. What is really needed is a date that makes you work.

Even in the case of long-term goals that might take a year or even multiple years to complete, you can still give yourself small interim goals that break up the time in between. I am a big fan of setting ninety-day goals. I believe that anything can be achieved in that time frame. A lot of the biggest successes I've had in my life have been in cycles of ninety days. Once I've decided what I want to do and I attach a date, it encourages me to give it all my time and effort until it comes to fruition.

I often compare my goal setting strategy to planning a wedding. If you were getting married and you already had a date set, the invitations are out and the RSVPs are coming in, you would do everything in your power to make sure all preparations are complete by the time the organist is playing "Here Comes the Bride." There isn't a bride on Earth who would send out the following invitation:

You are cordially invited to my wedding. I don't really know when it is, but I'll let you know eventually. All dates are subject to change, and they definitely will if things don't go as expected. We hope to see you there whenever we get around to it.

If you were to receive even one guest RSVP after an invite like that, I'd applaud you. The truth is nobody in their right mind would show up.

The world is starving for leaders who know exactly where they are going and is constantly searching for those who are willing to pave the way first. Leading from the front is key. A hard deadline shows everyone who sees it that you are taking things seriously. A good leader goes first for the sake of the team. When you can see an exact date, it will make you do the work. However, when you'd rather sit on the couch and binge Netflix or scroll instead, your deadline will make you get back into the mode of a wedding planner. I believe that all great things in life have a deadline for a reason. It's like you're telling the world,

"This is the plan. I'm prepared to back myself."

Or, in the case of our friend the platform diver,

"Look out world, here I come!"

My goals that I will achieve, because I believe:

GOAL:_____ DATE:_____

GOAL:_____ DATE:_____

GOAL:_____ DATE:_____

GOAL:_____ DATE:_____

GOAL:_____ DATE:_____

GOAL:_____ DATE:_____

GOAL:_____ DATE:_____

Just imagine what you could do if you actually went all-in and believed in yourself. The hair drenching wet, mascara running kind of ALL IN!

14

AFFIRM WHAT YOU WANT

The most successful people I know have one recurring thing in common: When you visit their homes, their entire living space is basically a pre-show for whatever it is they want. They have their desires written on signs and scribbled on mirrors. They keep model jets and pictures of their dream home posted up in laminated and framed prints on their walls. I do the exact same thing, as I've found that it is one of the stand-out secrets to success that I've come across. Someone unfamiliar with the reason behind this might wonder why, but the surprising thing is that it is one of the most psychologically powerful ways to achieve what you want. Our goals live and die based on whether or not we are affirming them. We literally have a responsibility to speak life into our goals and speak what we want over ourselves.

I have been known to stop what I'm doing, crank up my favorite song and have a full-on celebration over whatever it is I'm working towards at the time. It may not even be completely finished, but I make it a point to celebrate my goals and affirm them as if they are already done.

One of my favorite affirmations that I frequently use is, *I am creating a reality where I/that...*

What comes after "I/that" could be anything at all, as long as you phrase it as something already completed.

I am creating a reality where I am making $_____ a month.
I am creating a reality where I am energetic and full of vitality and passion.
I am creating a reality where I am a 6/7 figure coach/business owner/leader.

You get the idea.

The truth is that this has worked with every goal I have done it with. When you say it, you hear it, when you hear it, you believe it, and when you believe it, you can make it a reality. The sheer power of declaring your goals as already done is truly staggering. The reason I use the "I am creating a reality" method is that sometimes if we just use overly broad statements, for example, "I am the CEO of my company" or "I am making $250,000 or $1 Million a year," your subconscious mind might reply, "No you are not!" I get it. This might happen. But who really likes a backseat driver? What this affirmation does is open your subconscious mind to the idea that you are on a course towards your goal. It gives your subconscious mind permission to acknowledge that your time is coming and to accept it consciously.

By affirming yourself and your ability to create a reality in which your dreams are possible, a reality in which your goals are already done, you are engaging with one of the most powerful ways to get what you want. I typically have five things that I'm affirming at any given point. I like to work on my goals in sets of five because it forces me to focus on a limited set of things for a concentrated amount of time. I'd much rather juggle five goals confidently than attempt to juggle forty-seven and drop most of them. Once I've identified those five epic things that I want, I make sure to shower them with love, gratitude, and belief until I see them come to fruition.

Imagine what you could achieve if you could grasp the fact that you shape your own reality every day by what you affirm. The things that you speak to and affirm will ultimately grow. You're the one at the helm of it all, the one calling all the shots. Feel empowered by this. Whatever it is, make it specific, make it yours, make it what you want, and date it!

Then put it everywhere, say it daily, five times a day, and watch your dream life create itself before your eyes.

Affirm what you want using the statement: "I create a reality where I am...."

See page 185 for a list of example affirmations you recite to yourself to begin your affirming journey.

Now choose your top five goals that you want to manifest now, put on your favorite song and play it loud! Have a celebration while saying your affirmations and enjoy the feeling of it already being done.

The most important
words you speak are those
that come after this:
I am creating a reality
where I am....

15

YOUR VISION ENVIRONMENT

Abrief word on vision boards:
I freaking love them.
I can say with a fair degree of confidence that I consider myself to be a vision board expert. Personally, I don't have just one, but several in different forms. At home, I have one on a big poster board that I hang on my wall. On this, I've pinned meaningful photos, affirmations, and visuals that remind me of my goals. The layout and pictures change every six months to a year. Since the big goals are the ones that take the longest, I also like to take alternate approaches to my vision boards by spreading them out over the entirety of my various living spaces. But because I travel quite a lot, I can't take an entire house's worth of signs, pictures and my infamous post-it notes with me.

Or can I?

One of my favorite things to do is to help people build their own vision boards more effectively. In an ideal world, I'd gather all my readers into one big classroom to teach a course called, "Cassandra's Tips for Advanced Vision Boarding," or something to that effect. But, since I can't do that, let's call this a remote course. Over the years, I've come up with a number of different tricks to free my vision boards from being just a scrapbook, and all of them can be done on the go. When it comes to ways I visually represent my goals, I have three primary ways that I love to go about it:

Tip 1: Make it Portable - Like I was saying before, I love to take a ton of photos. One of the ways I make this work for me is by collecting all the pictures of things that I love and having them laminated. That way when I'm traveling and I need to stay in a hotel or apartment, I have them ready to set up wherever I am. You should always be prepared to surround yourself with things that reflect what you want and the key feelings associated with all of them. What you see daily dictates your vibration. When you are in direct control of what passes your vision, you can ensure that your goals are always being affirmed. What your mind sees is what you bring into your life.

Tip 2: Keep it to Yourself - Another way I maintain a vision board while on the move is through a private Instagram feed that is only for me. It's private and has no followers but by my current count there are over a thousand photos on there. These photos are like affirmations in and of themselves. But I usually go a step further and write a caption that affirms the photo's subject as already done. For example, I might upload a photo of a particularly gorgeous house accompanied by the caption: *I am creating a reality where I am living in this home with my beautiful family.* This could work with any affirmation you want.

Over time, you might even come across things you posted ages back that you didn't remember you'd already accomplished. I usually reserve my bigger, long-term goals for my wall, but my private Instagram feed is perfect for things I love and desire. By doing this, you're creating a future feed, a collage from which to feel your desires into existence, and best of all, the process is so much fun! The next time you have a few minutes and you catch yourself about to scroll the 'gram, switch to your private account and scroll through your vision instead. This is a *much better* use of time.

Tip 3: Create a Vision Video - Another unique way to create a vision board is by making time capsule videos that you can play at the end of the year. In my case, I tailor each video to be a celebration of everything I've been working towards. It may feel a bit strange leaving a message for yourself, but I promise you, you'll get the hang of it and it's a whole lot easier than you think. It is You you're talking to, after all. Some of my videos have "scripts" like, *Cass, it's the last night of the year and as we close it out together, we did it! We got the job, and the contract is signed. Right now, I'm in our dream home celebrating everything we've been working so hard for. Hooray, this one's for you.*

I film all of my videos like this, seated in front of my vision board so I can state each of my affirmations as real. You don't even have to wait until the end of the year to watch it. Any time you might feel discouraged or you are in need of a pick-me-up, play your video. There is so much power in believing when you hear your own voice.

When building your different vision boards, you really need to go all-out with it. Fill them with things that make you feel alive, things that bring your dreams to life. The more consistent you become in doing this, the more you will begin to see your environment shift. If ever you should find yourself deflated or struggling to believe, look back to the boards that you've built. Realign with your vision and hear the truth in your own voice:

"You know what? It's done."

Create your Vision Environment:

1. Make your vision board on the wall or a vision Instagram and start posting along with the verbiage that shows it is done.

2. Make a real-life vision board.

3. Put your signs up to make your vision environment come to life.

4. Make a vision video that you will play at the end of the year.

5. Turn your home into a living vision environment.

The answer to all you desire,
and all you want, is found in
your VISION or lack of it!

Make your VISION crystal
clear and fall in love
with what you see when
you close your eyes!

16

THE VISION BEYOND
THE VISION

Allow me to share a secret with you:
Your Ego is an absolute coward.
No, seriously. The closer you get to achieving your goal, the more your Ego will begin to perceive this as the end of its life. Let me tell you, the last thing it wants is to die. It genuinely sees you achieving your goals as its death, so it will do anything to protect itself. Success and checking off your mental goal list can send your Ego into an absolute panic. What it wants more than anything is to keep you "safe," (or at the very best its closest and best approximation of what it thinks "safe" is) and it will do anything and everything in its power to prevent you from branching out in your achievements. So, what can we do to put our ego at ease?

The answer lies in creating a vision beyond the vision.

Sometimes when people are so focused on just what they want, it can create a tunnel-vision effect, as if they are going along their path with blinders on. What this really stems from is a subconscious fear of achievement. Our poor Ego knows that once that ultimate desire is realized, it's game over. There's nowhere left for it after that. We can combat this, however, by creating a life plan.

Our day-to-day goals, the ones we're working at right this minute, are usually ones that will be accomplished in a shorter amount of time. Some might take ninety days, others might take a year, or some might be done by the time you finish reading this book. But beyond that, we need longer-term goals as well as the more immediate ones. Once again, let's picture ourselves at the riverbank across from the celebratory bash we imagined earlier. What did you see on that other side? How did you feel?

Whatever it was is your destination.

One of the many ways I hone in on this is by writing a future letter to myself. Some might call it a five-year plan, but I write mine as a sincere letter describing where I want to be, what it will look like, what it will feel like, and what life will be like when I get there. What this actually does is make your Ego feel safe and it will subconsciously encourage it to help you, rather than hinder you. Because it now knows that the next goal isn't the end, there's still the next one, and the one after that. There are five more years of goals to chase. Or it doesn't even have to be five years. It could be a letter setting up goals for the next twenty years into the future. The key is to always keep this letter with you. Fold it up and keep it in your wallet, purse, or pocketbook. When you go back to it, treat it like a roadmap that leads to wherever it is you're headed. My letter to myself is personally one of my favorite possessions. It reminds me of where I'm going and how I intend to get there, and the only thing I have to do, if ever I feel even a little bit lost, is to take another look into my future.

Challenge 16

"My Vision Beyond the Vision"

Declare your five-year vision:

Write a future letter to yourself, frame it and sit it on your bedside table. Read it every evening before sleep.

It is the BIG VISION we are creating. If we are going on a journey, it's not the road bumps and detours it's the final destination that matters! DECLARE where you are headed!!

People follow people that KNOW where they are GOING!

17

EMBRACE THE JOURNEY

I love a good, extended metaphor.
As you may have already noticed, using metaphors is one of the ways I like to contextualize things for myself. I teach in stories as it's one of the most effective ways I've found to put things in perspective and have an easy understanding of what I'm dealing with at any given time. One of my favorite analogies is what I like to call my Vehicle to Success.

Here's how to make one for yourself:

The Vehicle and The Sat-Nav

Start by determining what kind of car it is (not that it matters, but it's a free imaginary ride, so why not go with something you love?). Once you have that decided, the next thing you need is a destination, right? We've again returned to our metaphorical riverbank, across from which is our to-die-for metaphorical party, so this is the destination that you could plug into the sat-nav first. Or maybe you can try somewhere new. This sat-nav is represented by your mind and truly what you want.

Once you've determined where you're headed and what you really want, then you need to lock it in. This requires the same level of unconditional trust and faith that you would have in an actual sat-nav. When you punch in the directions for any trip, you may find that the road ahead does not look like what you expected. But you still have faith that it will get you to your destination no matter what. The existence of a sat-nav doesn't necessarily negate the existence of detours or a missed turn or two, but it will accommodate for those obstacles and it will reroute you to your destination.

Fuel / Gas - This Is Your Why

The fuel, in the case of your metaphorical car, is your "why," or the reason behind your journey in the first place. Your "why" is the most important part of all of this. You can say you want something, and you can even have a vision board, but, if you don't know why you want it, there will never be enough fuel in the tank for you to commit to the work.

Take time to consider why you're striving for your goal. Don't worry about how you'll get there. If you spend too much time agonizing over the "how," you won't go anywhere. The answers will come in time. Instead, focus on the specific reasons why your dreams are so important. This will give you direction and drive when it is time to make moves.

Why I do what I do is to ultimately impact one billion lives by giving people the power to believe in themselves. This is what drives me in all of my endeavors. Because I am so passionate about my reason for believing, any speed bumps I encounter are all minor. They're all a part of the journey because I know why my goal is important.

Ask yourself, what is your "why?"

Lights - Your Vision

The next most important thing when you're driving to your vision is to ensure that the lights work. Have you ever had your headlights go out and have to drive in the dark? It's terrifying. When your vision is obscured, how on earth could you expect to get anywhere? But when your high beams are on, you can drive with confidence and can respond to any obstacle in your way. The same is true with your destination. You need to have a crystal-clear vision of where you're going and what it looks like. This vision needs to be so compelling that it pulls you like a magnet towards it. This is the main thing that is going to get you excited to go above and beyond. When the vision you hold for you, your family and your life is clear, you will do whatever it takes.

Tires - Your Personal Development

I don't have to explain what these are for, do I? Like fuel, you aren't going anywhere without four inflated tires. In the case of this metaphor, think of this as your personal development and growth. Everyone believes, perceives, and projects based on what they're reading, what they're listening to, and whom they're spending their time with. This is what in essence, puts the air in our tires. No one can ever really know when they're going to get a flat tire, but it's usually when you haven't pumped in some air in a while. Personal development is the air. Each day when you do something to expand your mind and heart, you are topping up your tires. Hitting a massive bump in the road with a low tire will do the obvious and likely leave you stranded. Now compare that to hitting a speed bump with strong tires that are full. You'd hardly notice the bump, right?

Quality personal development that strengthens your mind-set will get you through anything. I feel the most valuable asset a person can possess is a rock-solid mindset. Whether it's reading ten pages of a good book a day, or playing a short podcast during your commute, you are creating a university on wheels. Just as long as you are learning every day and broadening your horizons, you will enhance your experience. It will make your journey smoother and you'll be able to travel undeterred because you have a strong, resilient vehicle supporting you. It all comes down to the power of personal development. It truly is like air in your tires: you can't see it, but you can tell if it is there or not.

Steering Wheel - Your Goals

In the same way that your steering wheel literally directs the car where it needs to go, the same is true of the smaller goals along your journey. To get from where you are to where you want to be, you need to know your destination and goals.

Having goals without direct planning or deadlines is the same as planning a trip with no direction or intention to even steer the car. You are the one who has to grip the steering wheel. Nobody else can do it for you. Maybe in your life, there are others vying for the wheel when you are supposed to be the only one holding it. What are your top five goals to accomplish in the next three to six months? What are the steps that will take you closer to your destination?

The Accelerator - Your Inspired Action

Last, but certainly, not least is the car's accelerator. In life, this is your inspired action. Absolutely nothing can happen without it. You can have the most amazing car in the world—polished up, full tank of fuel, but if you don't put your foot down on the accelerator, you aren't going anywhere. Ask yourself this: do you know where you are going? Do you know what your next steps are? If you do, then take decisive action and move forward. The only person who can ultimately propel you to your destination is you. What are the key action steps you need to take daily for your business, career, and life moving forward? Get started and do it daily. We start because we are committed, and we finish because we are consistent. Get yourself out there.

Good things come to those who go for it.

Draw or describe your dream car and how its various parts all add to your specific goals.

You are the vehicle to your success, fuel it with the strongest WHY!

18

ENHANCE SELF-CONFIDENCE

I began this book by introducing you to your Future Self. I hope you've kept your meeting at the front of your mind because there's a reason why we started there. It's the same reason why I encourage people to do this visualization all the time. This is because actively envisioning where you want to be is one of the most effective ways to build confidence.

When you imagine your ideal future, you aren't merely daydreaming. You're actually doing something called "visioneering" when you picture yourself living out the things you want to do. The true key to believing in yourself is having the confidence to say your goals are already complete. Once you do that, you can take action. If you put the work in, you will get what you want. EVERY TIME! Confidence can only come from staying true to your word. There is nothing quite like being able to say, "I did what I said I would." Committing yourself to follow through will make you more aware of what you give your word to. When you commit to something, you are more likely to follow through every time, and when you are persistent in keeping your word, you will continue to build confidence in your ability to deliver.

Something people don't realize is that not honoring your word can affect your level of self-worth. Letting yourself down is actually harmful to you. Not following through on your word can be self-betrayal and a form of self-abandonment. When you know you will back yourself and follow through, your confidence will soar. Honoring your own word and seeing things through will further validate all of your affirmations. It matters that you prove to yourself that you are good at what you do. This is called increasing your self-efficacy, or the belief in your ability to get something done. Even though you might have high self-confidence overall, you can have low self-efficacy in things you don't typically do. There's no shame in not having enough experience in something. That doesn't mean you can't be proud of the things that you *can* do. When you have self-efficacy backed by action, you can achieve whatever it is you set out to do. At the end of the day, all we have is our word. It is a representation of who we are as people. What we say we become, so what are you committing to on a daily basis and following through on or not?

What I want for you, however, is for you to be able to start being proud of the things that you do. I want you to be able to look at yourself and say, "You know what? I'm getting better every day. I have good sense of self-confidence and self-efficacy in what I do." That recognition is what is going to help you back yourself. When you have that self-confidence backed by action, you'll truly believe in yourself and know you can achieve whatever it is you set out to do.

You've seen it. It is already done, and you are constantly moving towards it.

The truth of the matter is, all we have is our word. Our integrity and capacity for follow-through are both our greatest possessions and our best motivating tools. Our integrity is our word, and our word represents us. I can guarantee that you'll find yourself surprised at how being aware of what you say "yes" to, and then acting on it with grace, will boost your level of self belief. Knowing what you want, holding the vision, and taking aligned action is going to get you what you want every time. When it comes to saying yes, remember:

If it's not a full-body "Yes," then it's a "No."
Own your "Yes" and your "No" and be proud.
Make your Yes mean YES and your No mean NO.

Our integrity and capacity for follow-through are our best tools in building confidence and our ability to believe that we can make things happen.

Decide on something that you want to accomplish today, commit to it, and see it through. Afterwards, write about how it made you feel to stick to your word.

What are some other things this week that you today will 100% commit to following through on?

FEELINGS can fade.
Commitment is saying YES
then following through on
what you said you would do
long after the feeling has gone.

Ready is not a feeling,
it is a DECISION!

19

CREATE AND DRIVE ACTION

I f there's one thing I know about my readers and supporters it's that they are without a doubt, achievement-oriented folk who want to win at life. I am sure you are no different. I am confident that you are willing to put in the work to make your desires a reality.

Now is the time for you to take daily decisive action toward your goals. At this point in your journey, your most important task is being self-aware and making sure your actions are in service of your desired result. This is your chance to do what you love and keep doing it. Ask yourself, *am I going to walk out of this month with a good story or a good excuse?* If you're wondering what your next course of action should be, then take a look at your situation and react with certainty.

Get it done.

Any action is better than no action at all.

Another excellent way to gain direction is to write down what you're good at, do more of it, then delegate whatever it is you don't particularly love to do. This could be by hiring an assistant to help you with administrative tasks or even just asking your children to help you with chores around the house. Anything that can save time and energy will begin to attract more of the same in amazing and surprising ways. Do what you do best and delegate the rest. Delegating doesn't always have to cost you either.

I learned the art of delegation at the age of seven. One weekend, my dad asked me to pull up the weeds along the walkway that stretched between our barn and the house. He offered to pay me the large sum of five cents per weed (what a deal!). Of course, the young entrepreneur that I was, I decided to employ my four-year-old brother to help me. Many hands make light work, right? I offered to pay him one cent per weed. It was pure genius (well, I thought, sorry Dorian). The moral of the story?

Work smarter, not harder.

If there's one thing I've learned, it's that people genuinely love to help and support others on their journey. This is why I love bringing my family and friends into the process of my vision boards. They know the reasons behind my goal. When you allow those close to you to add to the vision, you are giving them an opportunity to move with you towards the goal.

As you continue to engage with what you love and delegate what you don't, you will eventually find out what you're good at. Once you've identified what I call your "zone of genius," do as much of it as possible. The more work you do in your zone of genius, the more successful you will be in all areas of life. If your time is an investment, acting in your place of power is going to give you the greatest return on it. Plain and simple. The most vital resource you have in life is your time, and where you put it determines your results. Consistency over time is the key.

It is important that you care about whatever you are doing. When you love what you do and you get help with the rest, you will find that life will be considerably smoother, and you will be in a better alignment to attract even more of what you love.

Doing what you love is never a waste of time.

"DRIVE AND ACTION"

What is my genius? What is my point of power?

What am I willing to delegate?

What will this allow me to do more of?

Why is it worth doing more of what I love?

NO ONE that did the work didn't MAKE IT!

20

RELEASE RESISTANCE
TO RECEIVING

You deserve to receive all that you desire. Full stop. Sometimes the greatest givers often find it very hard to receive. I'm sure we've all known someone who is always giving selflessly regardless of what they have, yet seem incredibly resistant to receive anything in return. I've always lived by the principle that as much as you give, will be directly proportionate to what you are able to receive. As much as you can receive, you will be able to give. It is important to embrace both evenly and your life will be one of abundance. If you truly want to be able to give effectively, you have to develop the ability to receive so that your cup is always full. Genuine giving will only enhance your own receiving. Whether we realize it or not, sometimes we can develop a subconscious resistance to great things happening to us.

Allow me to release you from that. Be free.

I personally believe that 80% of success is based on one's mindset, belief, vision and faith. The remaining 20% is literally just aligned action. No matter what may be going on in your life at any particular time, get into the habit of asking yourself the following questions:

1. What's going well for me today?

2. What is good about these things?

3. What do I love in my life right now?

These questions will shift your mindset into "receiving mode," allowing you to see more abundance in your life. Because when you see more abundance, you'll see more success and allow more success into your life.

The key thing about releasing your resistance to receiving is recognizing the overflow in your own life. This will continue to allow you to bless others through what you have received and share your success with those who are around you. Being acutely aware of how good things are for you will help you to be humble and have a coachable spirit. Someone who is willing to learn will always be reminded of what they have. In order to have more of anything, you need to have an appreciation for what you've already got. You can't hate what you have now and vibrationally attract something better.

Your life will begin to change when you truly realize that you can be a magnet for miracles, if you allow it.

Gratitude is an attitude. You can choose it moment by moment.

What is going well for me today?

What is good about these things? Why am I so grateful?

What do I love in my life right now?

Your capacity to RECEIVE equals your capacity to GIVE!

Be known for your LOVING!

To LOVE someone is to BELIEVE in them.

21
CONSISTENCY AND FAITH

Here's a thought:

Anything you're good at is only because you do it all the time. If you're a good cook, it's not because you saw a high-res photo of ratatouille once and suddenly knew all the techniques to recreate it. If you're a good parent, it's not because you only decide to look after your little ones once or twice a year when the inclination strikes. If you're a good musician, it's not because you heard John Coltrane's "Giant Steps" playing in the background of a Macy's one afternoon. No one has ever become an expert at something overnight.

Someone who is incredibly wealthy is likely making weekly investments. Someone who is really fit is probably working out daily. Everyone with a high success rate in something has one very specific thing in common: they are incredibly consistent. If I could boil down all we've covered so far into one thing, it would be that the compound effect is the greatest asset on your journey to success.

The compound effect, taught best by Darren Hardy, is anything that you do daily, even for a short time. It is so crucial that many have proclaimed it "The Eighth Wonder of the World". Consistent, repetitive practice in a skill is like depositing a dollar in your bank account every day. Each moment-to-moment investment is small, but over a long period of time you will see it compound greatly beyond where you started. The same is true of your skills. If you put a small amount of work in every single day, you will acquire what Jeff Olsen refers to as the "slight edge." It is the application of that edge that helps experts become successful in their fields.

If you asked me what my number one tip for success is, I would impress upon you that consistency is the real key. Throughout my career, my personal edge is that I always aim to be the most consistent person in the room. Believe me, I have watched it compound greatly over time.

You can have that too.

Challenge yourself to be the most consistent person in the room. Make the decision to invest in yourself by dedicating an hour a day towards working in your area of genius. Whether that's thirty minutes in the morning and thirty minutes at night, find some time during your day to make that investment in yourself. If you are able to maintain the course and continue to compound those personal investments, I can promise you that when you look back, you will see great results.

In addition to consistency, the last thing you need for success is unconditional, unwavering faith. The most imperative currency for success is a strong work ethic. When you combine that with faith, you will absolutely receive what you desire.

Consistency is key, but it can be a challenge. You will only be as consistent as your passion for your vision and desire. A fantastic way to help yourself maintain this consistency and meet the challenge is by keeping a diary or planner to block out the time you need. Plan out your course of action, decide what you want to work on, and then commit to it.

When I journal out my plans, I often like to separate my different responsibilities into categories. The fixtures in my schedule that are absolutely immovable, I mark in red. Things like family time, religious time, and personal commitments are things I don't mess around with. Those are the things I do not move no matter what. Personal things such as fitness classes, leisure activities and just general things I love are marked in blue, and those are dotted in between my main tasks. The last pen I use is green, because as I always say, green means go. These are my opportunities to do pockets of business. Sometimes this is in four slots of fifteen minutes or a ninety-minute chunk of time during the day. It typically varies based on what I have on my plate at the time. No matter what, I make sure to block things out accordingly so that when the time comes to do the work, I treat it as a commitment. I'm less likely to put it off or procrastinate because I know the value assigned to that time. I am willing to make that daily investment. It's vital to have these times scheduled because knowing exactly what you're going to do and when you're going to do it will immediately motivate you to make the best use of your time.

Think back to the dream that you've been holding onto all this time. You've already given yourself radical permission to go all out for it, to truly put in the work that's necessary to get what you want. When you are consistently repeating the same action through a commitment to the work, you will be able to look back to find that it has compounded so much more than if that time was wasted elsewhere. It's that commitment to returning to the task that is the true slight edge. It is what creates genuine leverage and will be what brings you the most success.

From here on out, it's about the work. It's about falling in love with the slight edge, compounding your actions, and being consistent. If you can master this, you will be able to perfect what it takes to be a winner at anything you set your mind to.

I commit to doing the following things consistently:

The most consistent
person always **WINS!**

22

TURN COMPARING INTO BELIEVING

If the best part of everyone's life is their own personal story, why is it that we so often compare ourselves to others? This is something that I'm still working on myself and I'm sure many others can relate to as well. Comparison, in truth, is the thief of all joy. Contrasting your journey with someone else's makes it impossible to fall in love with all the beauty in your own life. In order to truly enjoy your life for what it is, you have to let go of being worried about what other people are doing.

No matter what your role is in life, you are incredible and unique for a reason. Your individuality is what makes you powerful. The whole world is looking for you to step into your own shoes and really take ownership of your story, your power, your strengths and your weaknesses. The world is waiting for you to own it all. How much longer are you going to wait before you step into your sovereign power and completely own your story? Your story is what makes you vulnerable, authentic and breeds connection. Real connection at that! When we step into our authentic power, it allows us to better connect with others. At the end of the day, that is what everyone wants–to connect. Ridding ourselves of façades and artifice allows the world to see us in our true glory, and in turn, allows us to see the world in a new, more beautiful way.

It is vitally important that we break the cycle of comparing ourselves to others because it's really a game we will never win. There are so many negative effects that come with this trap. Sometimes, I honestly cringe when I hear people compare themselves to others. No two people are the same and no two people are on the same journey. We all need to see ourselves in our own individual space and allow others to show up as their best selves as well.

When we get stuck in the comparison trap, we can become victims of negative and anxious thoughts. This can be a really hard cycle to break out of and it can show up in our lives in many different ways. For some, it appears as anxiety or depression, for others, it may manifest as overspending or a strong compulsion to keep up with the Joneses. Some might try to satisfy their urge to compare themselves with others through their online presence, but as studies have shown, many people feel worse about themselves after spending large amounts of time on social media. What these individuals fail to realize, however, is that negativity, overspending, and obsessing with how they measure up to others takes a toll on their mental health as well as their bank accounts. Over the years, I've learned six practical steps to stop comparing myself with others that I want to share with you.

My first tip is this, one of the habits that changed everything for me is being present in the moment and expressing gratitude. The way I go about doing the former is by focusing on what I can taste, smell, see and hear in order to bring me into that present moment. Sometimes we can find ourselves going through life on autopilot. We've all spaced out on a commute and arrived at our destination with no clear memory of how we got there. When I catch myself doing things like this, I turn my attention to my senses. I ask myself, "What does the wheel feel like in my hands? What can I hear? What do I smell?" Focusing on the details of the moment is a powerful tool to carry with you everywhere. Practicing gratitude, an equally important step, is most easily done when you're in the moment. In addition to using your senses to identify the details of the present, you can also focus on the things in your life that you're thankful for. Tip two, take the time to remind yourself of the blessings in your life and allow yourself to recognize them as truly special. When you stop to think about it, you'll realize that you have so many things to be grateful for. This will release you from feeling the need to look at others out of the corner of your eye and compare yourself to them. When you are focused on what you are grateful for at that moment, you won't feel the need to redirect that focus elsewhere. A good way to keep your blessings in mind is to write them down. Keep an ongoing list of the things that you are thankful for, in your phone or in a notebook, and add to it when good things happen. They don't even need to be anything particularly grandiose. Instead, develop the skill of finding simple expressions of gratitude, no matter what they may be for, and keep them on your mind. As you continue to watch your list grow, you can enjoy the satisfaction of being grateful in whatever situation you find yourself in.

The best thing about making a daily practice of expressing gratitude is that it brings about the next step in our process—embracing contentment. What this does is allow you to be in a state of joy, appreciation, satisfaction, and anticipation for the things you want, no matter what your present circumstances are. If you are happy with who you are and what you're doing, you won't feel the need to endlessly line up your life with everyone else's to see how they compare. So often, we worry over what people are thinking about us when in reality they're probably thinking about their place in their own journey. Instead of wasting your energy over stressing over the opinions of others, you can instead focus on becoming at peace with your current life and developing a sincere enjoyment of what you're doing. We can't base our happiness on what we hope to achieve tomorrow. We need to base our joy on what we have right now at this moment. Tomorrow is never guaranteed, and you can't afford to let your journey pass you by without seeing the beauty in it.

My third tip is to avoid comparing your real life with everyone else's highlight reels. In a world of Instagram and Facebook stories, it is very easy to see other people's lives and assume they are better off than we are. You might see a photo on social media of something extravagant and think, "I'm not there yet," when most times, people are only posting their best photos, experiences, and stories. A highlight reel doesn't take into account the entire picture of someone else's life. We all go through our various experiences in different cycles and seasons. The low points in your life may coincidentally be high points in others' lives and vice versa. We frequently spend too much money and emotional energy to keep up with a life that we think everyone else is living, but in turn, we end up missing out on the things in our life that are going well for us. I encourage you to shift your focus off of what others have going on and instead water your own lawn. When you do that, you'll be able to turn things around for yourself.

This brings us to our fourth tip, which is to maintain focus on your strengths and remain humble. One important thing to note is that you don't need to beat yourself up to be humble. In fact, it's almost impossible to do both. When we are confident in our strengths and approach them with humility, we are actually creating a space for other people to believe in themselves. Confidence coupled with humility is the evidence of believing in your inherent worth. Being overly critical of yourself robs you of the chance to feel good about your unique strengths. Sometimes, the more we compare ourselves to others, the worse we feel about ourselves. This is a dangerous place to be. We need to avoid beating ourselves up over our perceived flaws and instead direct our attention towards the things that we bring to the world. Identify what you're proud of and write them down. Those are your gifts. Make sure to remember them.

Tip five, celebrate. When I'm looking at others and their accomplishments, I don't look to compare myself with them. I look to see what's possible and then I celebrate them knowing that I'm next. Constantly comparing yourself to others without celebrating is a trap. Instead, you can actually compare in a healthy and productive way. I like to look at where people are at and think, "Wow, that's inspiring. Maybe I could do that, too." One of the healthiest habits to develop is the ability to derive inspiration from seeing others succeed rather than feel as if you are missing out. Begin to tell yourself, "If they can, I can," and believe in your ability to succeed at whatever you set your mind to. My challenge to you, is when a friend or a family member tells you about something that's good in their life, take part in their enthusiasm. Join them in their celebration and rejoice with them the way that you would want them to with you. Instead of comparing, I want you to be inspired. If someone shares something great with you, keep the focus on them instead of turning the focus back onto yourself. Turn your vision outwards, not inwards. If you can find big and small ways to celebrate other people's accomplishments, those accomplishments will become yours. I'm reminded of a verse in the Bible, Romans 12:15, which says to "rejoice with those who rejoice." You should never feel like you're losing out because someone else is winning. Neither your success nor theirs, have anything to do with each other. You are both separate entities, working towards your own individual successes. Remember the blood, sweat, and tears that went into your own work and celebrate others' accomplishments, knowing they put forward the same effort.

Tip six is to learn to compete with yourself instead of competing with those alongside you. Instead of focusing on where you are compared to others, compare yourself with where you were yesterday and decide to be even better tomorrow. Even if you become just 0.01% better, you're still growing. Keep a record of how you've progressed and compare that with where you want to be. Being able to see how much you've stretched, improved, and grown over time will give you the motivation to keep going.

The last thing to make sure you do is to develop some boundaries about how much time you're spending looking outwards. Whether that be looking at social media or looking at other people, comparison is something that you need to put the reins on. It's perfectly okay to look outward from time to time, as we've established that it can be a good source of inspiration but creating hard limits will allow you to create a healthy balance. One of the things that you can put in place, is to set a timer for scrolling. Give yourself a certain amount of time per day, and when it's done, walk away. In the evenings, try setting your phone to airplane mode. You can also reserve social media for just your computer, that way when you step away from your desk, you won't feel tempted to scroll excessively. Unfollow any accounts that don't make you feel inspired or cause you to compare yourself to others in a negative way. Don't always feel obligated to check in and be live daily on social media. You don't have to do that if you don't want to. Periodically, do a social media detox. Take a day off and focus on doing what you love. It's amazing to see how much time you have for other things when you don't fill every nook and cranny of your life with scrolling.

My desire for you is that you will be able to look back at your story, wherever you may be in it, and be able to feel pride. I want you to be able to celebrate the unique beauty of your individual journey and see the beauty in it. All it takes is just a daily, consistent effort, to shift your focus.

What are some practical ways in which you can turn comparison into self-belief?

Remember, if someone else has accomplished it, has it or has achieved it then you can too. If you can see it in others, you can see it within yourself.

Identify some key figures in your life to take inspiration from. What have they created that allows you to see that if they can, you can?

You have to own your story and stand in it. Or, you have to stand outside of it hustling for your worth.

Your story is a piece of art and so are you!

OWN IT!

23

BELIEVE IN YOURSELF

An undeniable truth is that we get what we think about on a subconscious level. Ask yourself, what are you expecting? So many times in life, we want something, we think we're going for it, but what we're actually doing is the opposite. We're speaking against it. We're acting and operating at a low vibration and we cannot work out why we can't have or get what we want. Have you ever been in a situation where you thought, "I really thought I was going to achieve that," or "I really thought I was going to have that," but deep down, you're also thinking, "I knew something bad was going to happen. I knew that the other shoe would drop. I knew that wasn't going to work out for me." Things like that are actually representative of your subconscious belief level. What we want to do is shift those thoughts and bring things back into alignment. This way, we can truly believe the same on all levels about all the things we expect.

Take some time and perform a belief audit. Ask yourself, what is your level of belief around your finances? What is your level of belief around your faith and spirituality? What is your level of belief around your relationships, your fitness, and your freedom? What is your level of belief around the things that you want? Because if we're not believing at the highest level, we're going to be attracting things that are subpar in comparison to what we want. All aspects of our lives come down to one thing, and that is our belief in ourselves and the level of worthiness and deserving that we hold for what we can have.

It takes some time to realize that we always get what we expect, whether we like it or not. Sometimes that can be hard to hear because our expectations and desires can be in conflict with one another. When that happens, we're out of alignment. We're vibrating in fear, doubt, and lack. So, if you're feeling good, you're in alignment with what you want and you're in alignment with what you expect.

A crucial point I want to share with you is to start believing in yourself from the place of knowing how good you are in the areas of your life that you're *already* confident in. Are you a great cook? Do you play an instrument? Are you an excellent mum or dad? What is it that you're really good at? Paying close attention to the things you're skilled at will continue to remind you of the ways in which you're consistent. Identify what the positive areas of your character are, and what you do in order to be good at them. Once you do that, I want you to transfer those skills into another area of your life.

For example, if you're really good at the gym, because you're consistent, you're passionate and hardworking, ask yourself what would happen if you took those key skills into how you manage your finances or your relationships? What if you took those skills into the way that you ran your family home or the way you run your business? I can tell you this, you would feel confident, and you would believe in yourself in those other areas of your life also.

One of the things I love most in this world is dance. I know I'm good at it. I'm passionate about it. I can walk into any class anywhere in the world and simply enjoy the experience of dancing. What I've done is take the skills that I have learned from that passion and transfer them into my businesses, finances, relationships, and friendships. The confidence and self-belief that I have as a dancer is something I can transfer into every area of my life. The reason I am very successful as a top 1% network marketing consultant is that I had businesses beforehand. I had business knowledge and had been a businesswoman for 10 years prior to starting in the industry. I took all of my previous experiences and the belief that I had in myself and transferred that to network marking. I thought to myself, "You know what? If I can do it here, I can do it there. If I can do it then, I can do it now." I urge you to find what you're really good at, own it, and believe in it.

Another thing to keep in mind is your self-talk. It is imperative that you make sure that you are breathing belief into yourself. Are you someone who says,

"I can..."
"I will…"
"I am…"
"I get to…"
Or are you someone who says,
"I should."
"I could."
"I would."
"I have to."

Take a moment to really examine how you speak to yourself. When you're thinking, "I want to enhance my finances" or "I want to enhance my relationship" I want you to say instead, "I get to enhance my relationship. I get to work on my finances. I get to save. I get to work out," and so on. Language changes everything. You've got to be aware of how you talk to yourself, because the most influential person you will listen to is you, and you need to be speaking belief and life over yourself. Your self-belief will come out in the way you speak.

Once you've taken care to change the way you speak, the next step is to visualize yourself, doing well in that area of life that you were struggling in before. If you're thinking, "I'm struggling with my finances," visualize yourself at the end of the year with savings and enough to afford the things that you love. What you desire is all out there. You've just got to attract it. Visualize yourself in that perfect relationship with your dream person, or with the beautiful family you've always wanted, or with perfect health. Know it, see it, and feel it. Once you are familiar with that feeling, go for it and be consistent.

When we say we get what we expect, what we're really saying is, we get what we believe. Many times, we forget that we can actually change what we expect by putting on a different lens. That begins with being persistent. The thing about persistence is, you are the creator of your life. You can create anything you want. Now, most of the time, when you have a really big vision, things are going to pop up and test you to see whether you really want it. Persistence, especially in situations like that, is everything.

I have a favorite saying from when I was training to be a dancer. *Persistence makes the impossible possible, the possible likely, and the likely definite.* So many people back down when they hear a "no," a "not yet," or some other kind of objection. When we come up against that objection, we are instantly inclined to change our vision. I'm encouraging you, to set the vision and lean on your power of persistence to create what you really want. I never think anything is impossible because I know that I've got the power of persistence within me. Persistence makes the impossible possible, the possible likely and the likely definite. Is a statement I have always believed. Every dance move I've mastered, presenting skill I have honed, and opportunity I have had in business has only been achieved to the level that I desired because I was relentlessly persistent! I encourage you to do the same because the power of persistence is something that you can cultivate and master. Most of all, it really makes you lean on that "no matter what" ideology. It creates a "whatever it takes" mentality. Persistence can also come from having a really big vision. If you light a fire under yourself by setting a massive vision, you will do whatever it takes to get there, because you want it so badly. You need to make sure that your goals are massive and meaningful. If you do that, no hurdle will be too big for you. The things that you love, the things that you want, and the things that are in your heart will always be things that you will move Hell or high water to achieve.

It is important to remember that you get what you expect. Bring your subconscious and conscious thinking in line with each other and really identify what you expect. What do you expect by the end of the year? What will your finances look like? What will your relationships and friendships look like? What do you expect to feel like when you wake up in the morning? Consciously setting your expectations is key. When you do this, you can achieve what you're believing in and not just what your subconscious mind is expecting.

Belief is the foundation for all the things that you want.

What is one key thing you're expecting this year? How can you shift negative expectations into positive ones?

Persistence makes the impossible possible, the possible likely and the likely definite.

24

STOP SEEKING EXTERNAL APPROVAL

You become the average of the people that you spend the most time with. So, who is in your circle? Are you satisfied with the people in it? If not, why? Be sure to remember, there are instances where we can't change our circle, but we can put up a bit of protection around ourselves. In a situation where I find myself in an environment that is unsupportive or of a low vibration, I choose to imagine myself inside a glass bubble. Think of it like a glass capsule, you inside it. Protected. Inside this bubble is pure white light that helps me serve the world better and be able to bring the most I can to the table. When I'm there, I'm sending love, I'm present and I'm listening. However, at the same time, I'm limiting what is being allowed to land. Any negativity, I allow to just ricochet off the glass.

In the same way, we can't expect flowers to grow in a harsh environment, we also can't be our truest, loving selves if our environment isn't supportive. That isn't something that we can always change, though. Some people work in a workplace that is not supportive or they may have family members that aren't as supportive as they'd like, but the best thing you can be is a beacon of love. Your job is not to engage, retaliate, nor fight back against things like that, but to just be love and light. Be grateful that you even have the experience to meet these people. The more love you are able to show in these environments, the more you will be able to focus on your goals.

So, what would you want your life circle to be like? Whom would you love to have in your inner circle? The individuals you spend the most time with will be the ones who impact whom you become. It is important that we are able to detach our dreams and desires from the approval of others. That's one of the most important questions to ask, "How can we stop seeking approval from others?" I'm going to give you five steps that I really love when it comes to releasing the need for approval. The first step is to recognize when you're seeking external approval. Self-awareness is the foundation to changing all behavior. We all seek approval in areas of our life where we don't feel as confident, or, we don't believe in ourselves as deeply. When you notice that feeling come up–instead of seeking external approval–I want you to tap into that little self, inside of you (the little child inside of you) and make him or her feel at ease. Tell yourself, *you're loved, you're whole, and you're safe.*

Whenever we are looking for external approval, it's because our ego is making us feel fear and we're either feeling unloved, unwanted, unsupported, or misunderstood.

When we get into a situation where we no longer approve of ourselves, we then look for others to approve for us. Take comfort in the fact that everyone out there is just as scared of you as you are scared of them. They're also looking for approval. They're also looking for validation. The best thing that we can all learn is to validate ourselves from the inside and have that chat with our little self, to simply love on them. Just remember your letter to your younger self from earlier. *It's all safe. I'm an adult now. We're all good. Everything is going to be okay. We are loved and supported and we're going to get through.*

The second step is asking yourself, what type of approval are you seeking? Is it that you want to be validated for what you've done? Is it that you're looking for it on social media? Is it what you're looking for from your boss? Do you think that you need to have the ideal partner or relationship to be happy? What is the level of approval you are seeking?

In truth, you are the one who needs to absolutely rely on yourself and give yourself the approval you seek. Instead of feeling disconnected, unfulfilled or unhappy, take full responsibility *for* yourself and how you feel *about* yourself. Build yourself up. If you need approval from your boss, why don't you approve of the work that you've done yourself? If you need approval on social media, why don't you get that same approval from yourself, instead of using likes to measure your self-worth? Instead of needing an ideal partner, why not become the ideal partner first? Rather than seeking what you want externally, learn to seek it from within. The answers are already within you. The best gift you can give yourself is that absolute approval from within.

The next step is to continue to use positive self-talk. The next time you catch yourself seeking approval from others, instead of beating yourself up, I want you to create positive statements in contrast to that. So instead of saying,

"I can't..." or *"I'm not..."*

you can say,

"I can. I will. It's okay to feel this way. I am growing and learning every day. I choose to give this my best shot. My personal best is enough."

Give yourself a break. As you're growing, learning, and going through new situations, it's absolutely fine to have these growing pains. They're actually good. They are signs that you are becoming a better version of yourself. But it's up to you to give yourself that stamp of approval through personal, positive talk. The most important person that you talk to daily is you. Speak truth over yourself. Give yourself the grace and freedom to learn. When you stumble, get back up. We all may fall down many times over, but we can always get up. Each time that we do, we get up better. Instead of beating yourself up, I want you to beat your own drum. Start to back yourself, become your own best friend and your very best support person.

The next step from there is to give yourself the approval and validation you're looking for by giving it to others. The key is to give out what you want back in life. If you want more love, instead of withholding it from others, love freely and share it with them. Recognize people for their accomplishments. Tell them what you think is great. I'm a big believer in speaking your truth. If you think someone's done well, tell them you think so. Let's make a culture where we give love and life to other people. The more love you give out, the more that will come back to you. Then that will help you to really start to see how powerful you are and that you are creating a culture of love, deserving, and backing each other. Your life is a mirror of how you're feeling and thinking about other people. You cannot judge others and expect them to love you. You've got to be what you expect. Make an effort to start mirroring what you desire for your life and what you desire from you inner circle.

It goes without saying that we are all growing. There's no judgment, and all feelings are welcome. Everything will begin to change when you create your reality by knowing that you are the mirror to your world.

Identify some ways in which you might be seeking external approval. Find three practical ways you can back yourself today.

BELIEVING IN YOU IS YOUR SUPERPOWER

25

UP YOUR BELIEF

One of the biggest *"Aha!"* moments that I've had in my career began with the realization that every-thing I was looking for was already within me. Very often I would go to events and opportunity meetings with very successful leaders, and I would always be looking for the "secret sauce". I was constantly searching for the secret of what I needed to do differently to succeed. When I came to the height of my career, I realized whatever I needed to succeed was already a part of who I am. It was the day that I became absolutely, unapologetically myself that my business soared. My inner strength, trust, and belief in myself were what really took things to the next level, and I want to help you tap into that same source. Sometimes we've got to find it by being quiet, by being still, and working on being mindful. But I believe that you can tap into it at any time through the power of self-belief.

The first thing is to ensure that you are realistic about your goals in a way that excites you. Even if I have a massive goal that some would consider unrealistic, I remain practical in those goals by being consistent every single day. Having those massive goals and those really exciting thoughts and pictures in your mind is only going to be achieved if you are realistic about them. Putting in the daily effort to work towards your goal is a powerful tool in achieving even your biggest goals.

Each day you need to do something that makes you really feel good about yourself. This will help you create healthy routines to create consistency. It will make you do the things every day that will help you to get closer to your dream. It will support you to show up for yourself and do the little things that you really don't want to do. You might not feel like doing the things that you have to do all the time, but it's deciding to do them no matter what, that makes all the difference. You have to base your activity on what you know and think, not just how you feel. If you only followed the way you felt, you wouldn't do anything. Because if we always only did the things we felt like, we'd literally be laying on a cabana by a pool and nothing would be happening. Instead, hold the huge vision, hold the huge desire, and take action daily. Get up and work towards it.

Every single morning when I get up, I write down the things that I must do that day to take my businesses forward. I create healthy routines, whether they be my morning routine, visualization, reaching out to people, connecting with others, or offering people opportunities. I have a structure throughout my day so that I'm realistic with achieving that huge goal. By doing those things daily, I'm actually able to feel great about myself. That is what builds my self-belief because then I know that I'm the one that I can back up and absolutely bet on. Really, it's my activity that's going to make these goals happen. When I'm doing what I say I'm going to do, I start to build confidence.

Confidence is something people say they want, but it really comes from doing what you said you're going to do. Long after the feeling is gone, doing what you said you're going to do daily is going to take you closer to your goals. When you do what you said you're going to do, you start to feel confident, and when you have confidence, you start to believe in yourself. When you start to believe in yourself, you have a bigger vision, and you can start to chisel out that crystal clear picture of what you want. You can be sure that every day as you're working, you're not just working towards a wish or a hope, you're actually creating your future. Having those healthy routines throughout your day is absolutely key to creating something really powerful, and having that self-belief, knowing that if you put your word to it, you can bet on yourself to do it. That is vitally important in all businesses, goals, and things that we achieve.

Your next step from there is to surround yourself with positive people. Find people that talk about life, success, ideas and opportunities. Engage with people who aren't complaining, blaming, or justifying. You've got to be so cautious of who you talk to. Now you might think, "I can't talk to that many people throughout the day." You might be busy at work, or you're in a situation where you're in lockdown, but the truth of the matter is the people that you surround yourself with aren't just limited to those you come into immediate contact with. It's the things you listen to, the books that you read, and the things that you see that also play a part in shaping you. Those are the things that can create positivity and fuel growth. When you're excited and you're seeing, hearing and reading things that excite you and inspire you, you're actually going to be more inclined to do the work. When we're surrounded with positivity, we can be grateful and excited for whatever comes next. In that state of mind, you want to be thinking about all the feelings that you wish to feel more of. Get a good book. Follow encouraging podcasts. Create an environment that keeps you enthusiastic about what you do.

Another thing you can make a habit of is sharing what you have to offer and developing a growth mindset. The best way to develop a growth mindset is to learn something and then teach it. Make it a point to give what you know away. When I wake up in the morning, I think to myself, "Okay, what more could I do today for myself, for my team, for my family, and for the greater community? What more can I do to take other people's lives forward? Who could I help?" I take the time to scroll through my Instagram or Facebook and I look for people that I can serve. I make it a daily task to look for people that I can help. If I see a person who is longing for support or help, I'll reach out to them. When people reach out to me, I make sure I'm there to help them. Giving away what you have will help to develop that growth mindset. But remember, when you give things away, you have to learn more. The reason I write books, courses, and podcasts is that the process ensures that I am continuing to level up. I make a practice of creating and learning, to constantly remain in a state of growth, so that I can better equip my team and be there for my friends and family. When you're giving away your time, you always have to be filling back up. That is the mindset that you need to remain in. That is the mindset that will make you read, plug in, and look for more. It will make you hungry to become a better version of yourself, because the bigger you are, the more capacity you will have in your mind. Share what you have to offer. Know that when you help other people, it will also raise your belief when you see people achieve things because of your support. The best way to build yourself up is to help other people.

Have you ever felt petrified of something you genuinely want to do? You know in your heart that it's what you truly want, but you're so scared to do it that you feel frozen in place. This is because our journey towards our desires is one of vulnerability. This is a space that we often try to avoid, but it is honestly where the magic happens. When you are vulnerable, you will be able to connect with yourself and other people. Everything you want is on the other side of fear. Everything you truly want is on the other side of believing.

From now on, reach for the stars. Feed your mind and face your fears.

Go for it. Shoot for the moon.

Go higher and bigger than you've ever gone before. Get out of your comfort zone.

All the good things that have happened in my life have come on the other side of a massive twenty seconds of courage and a big jump. It's just because I believed in myself that I did it. Facing your fears builds your belief muscle. Like any muscle, you've got to take it to the gym. The way you do that is by sometimes having to, figuratively speaking, lift heavy weights. The more you stretch out of your comfort zone and take bold leaps of faith, the more you'll get used to it. At a certain point, you'll honestly start to get a kick out of doing things that scare you, which will enable you to take even bolder steps towards your goal.

Don't be afraid.

Don't be scared to speak up and draw on your strength. Make a habit of doing and saying what you want. Ask for what you want. Be bold and proud of what your desires are. Don't just sit and wait. Become an active problem solver. Ask people how you can help them with what's going on for them. Be proud of your voice because it gives people permission to speak up as well. Ultimately, it's not our darkness that scares us, it's our light. How big we can get, and our untapped potential is what scares us. You'll be so surprised just how many people you can inspire by being bold, courageous, and humble. Be bold about what you stand for and what you want to create. Speak it into existence. The greatest tool you have for creation is your word.

One last thing I would encourage you to do throughout your journey of increasing your belief is to take care of yourself. Self-love is the basis of self-belief. Ask yourself what can you do to look after yourself? Whether it's waking up that little bit earlier and doing your morning routine, fitting in a workout class, or even just simply eating healthy. Take special care to be kind to yourself as you go forward, as this will create deep respect for yourself.

The aim of it all is to continually place yourself in the position to continually raise your self-belief.

Think about some ways you can raise your self-belief.

What are some good habits that you can form?

What are some ways you can go outside your comfort zone?

How can you better look after yourself?

The day you realize everything you are desiring is already within you, is the day your life will BEGIN!

26

YOUR DREAMS ARE WAITING
FOR YOU TO SHOW UP

When you think of the year ahead of you, ask yourself what you can do to ensure that it's a great one. I think the best way to do this (in any month of the year, really) is just to own it. If things play out in ways you didn't expect they are either protection and a redirection, there's no loss. You can always recreate things at any moment. I want to encourage you to reflect back on the resolutions, goals, and intentions that you set at the end of last year. How far have you come along with those things that you declared you would do?

I want you to really focus on how you want to show up in both your business and your life in the next thirty, sixty, and ninety days. I want you to think about that self-image, the way you want to look, the way you want to feel, the way you want to show up in a room, the way you want to speak, and the way you want to come across. Build discipline around commanding yourself to do what you know you want, and then follow through with it. Give yourself the freedom to, be, do, and have more. Know that discipline is what creates freedom. Pay close attention to your work ethic around what you want. Because when external things are changing and are out of our control, the one thing that we can control is ourselves and our commitment to the work. Your work ethic isn't just limited to your means of employment. It can mean so many things. It can mean how you're feeling about yourself, how you're working out, how you're showing up in your relationships, or how you're saving and managing your finances. Make sure to examine your work ethic in all the seven areas of life we previously covered.

You want to make sure that for the rest of your year (and your life) you take a real ownership mentality. What do I mean by that? Many years ago, my coach and mentor explained it best:

"You can either rent it or own it. You can either blame someone else when something goes wrong, or you can own it and take full responsibility."

When you rent something and something bad happens to it, whose responsibility is it? It's not yours. Rather it's the responsibility of the person that owns it. The lights go out, the stove breaks or the fan doesn't work, it's not your fault. It's the owner's fault. But when you have a full ownership mentality, even if it's not your fault, it's still your responsibility. What happens when you get into an ownership mentality is you start saying, "I'm going to really own this and run with it." So, I want you to speak life over your business; speak what you want, and you will get what you want. Speak light, not darkness.

Every new goal requires a new you. Are you propelled by fear or faith? Are you worried that you're not giving your best? Are you worried that you're not good enough? Are you worried that you're not worth following? So many times, we would not have the incredible opportunities that we have if someone else didn't have the courage to ask us. I want you to fall into that absolute, unconditional, faith and trust that you are in your present opportunity for a reason.

BELIEVE

Get out of the habit of saying your goals publicly, when in reality you're justifying, complaining, and blaming behind the scenes. Inside, we're secretly hoping that someone or something externally is going to come to save us and change everything. I am speaking to the powerful queen and king inside of you–you are the person that has to get up and save you. You're the person that has got to go and save your future, your life, and your business. Stop hoping and wishing that someone in your current team and your current life will pop up and save you. The biggest change will occur when you release this because let's face it, a princess is someone who sits in waiting. She's sitting there languishing, hoping someone will come and save her. A queen steps into her power and claims what she wants. A queen doesn't wait to be asked to be chosen. A king doesn't wait to be told what to do first. A queen chooses her tribe. A king doesn't stay down for long. A queen believes it's coming for her. A king no longer plays with their goals, he chooses them and owns them. A queen does not play with her dreams; she lives them.

I want you to think, "This is my chance to do something special." In the next five years, people will look back and they will ask how did you do it? You're going to tell them about this year–the year you're reading this now, and how you decided to make a change. When everybody else was distracted, nervous, and falling asleep, you chose not to focus on the things you couldn't control.

We need to choose to dive deep into our own lives and into our own goals and stop focusing on the uncontrollable. Focus on your work ethic in all seven areas of your life, your action towards what you desire, and your personal belief. Then take a step and write the following affirmation down somewhere:

I commit to getting rid of anything this year that does not serve me.

I want you to focus on being a leader in whatever business you're in, whether you're an entrepreneur in network marketing, whether you're a parent, whether you're a principal, whatever your area, focus on the leadership. Leadership means somebody has to lead the ship. Think of your life as an incredible cruise liner that you are the captain of. People will come on for days, some for weeks, some for months, and some will stay on for years. You have to lead your ship to where you want to go. The question is, though, where do you want to go? Only you can answer that for yourself.

I want you to release the habit of something not going right, and then subsequently finding an excuse as to why you lost. Instead, I want you to create the habit of winning, and then finding a way to win again. Be absolutely honest with yourself and consider if you are doing what you're supposed to be doing? Have you really been playing to win? Have you earned what you want? Or have you just been showing up, seat-warming and hoping someone saves you?

Release the excuses and absolutely step into your power. Everyone wants to be successful, decide that you're going to finally let yourself be.

I want you to whole-heartedly focus on the work. Listen, be coachable, teachable, and absolutely honor your mentors. Some people spend more time questioning what to do than actually doing it. I'm telling you to go for it. Stop second-guessing yourself and focus on your own personal development. When you start demanding more from yourself than anyone else, that's when I believe your life will finally change. That's when the good stuff happens. Instead of asking others to do it, ask yourself, "can I do it first?" Decide to believe in your greatness and society will believe it's possible. Stop worrying. Stop fretting over whether or not good things are going to happen for you. If you're going to win, stop looking sideways. Stop looking at other people's successes and wondering what's wrong with you, because there is nothing wrong with you. I'm telling you right now, stop wondering if this will work for you and wonder instead if you're *willing to do the work*. Stop wondering if it's going to work for you and ask, "am I willing to show up and help others do the work?" Do the things that your leaders are sharing with you because they are in their position for a reason. I want you to believe in yourself and learn how to believe in what you want. You cannot learn what you want by watching videos and pieces of training. You've got to absolutely jump in the pool. All-wet, mascara running, completely all-in.

I want you to own it today. Own your power. Own what you want and everything that you desire is on the other side of your beliefs. Ask and it will be given, seek and you will find, knock and it will open.

I believe in you.

Your dreams are waiting for you to show up.

How do you plan to own this upcoming year?

Create your thirty, sixty, and ninety day goals, then write them down somewhere easily visible.

LIFE is a YOU project!

27

SUCCESS IS LINKED TO YOUR ABILITY TO LOVE

One of the most important things that you can recognize is the power of love–in your business, in your life and in your relationships. I encourage you to see people through this lens. Everyone is special to someone else. Every person you cross paths with is someone's mother, father, daughter, sister, brother, son, niece, nephew, or cousin. So, let's treat every person we cross paths with as if they are someone special to us.

I always ask people when I'm dealing with business, a contract, property, or anything, "if I was your daughter, would you still suggest this? If I was your daughter, would you recommend moving forward?". This question completely shifts the perspective. People start to think, "Oh, you're not just a person out there. You're not just external. You're someone's Someone." Try to think of others with this perspective when you're with people all throughout your day. To the lady behind the counter: "This is someone's mother, someone's sister, someone's auntie, someone's wife." To the man in the store: "That is someone's father, someone's husband, someone's brother, someone's uncle."

People are out there trying to live their best lives, doing the best they can, and they deserve to be loved, looked out for, celebrated, and treated with their best interest at the forefront of our hearts. I'm all about loving each other, and really recognizing that this is a feeling of attraction. This is a feeling of the highest vibration. How we feel about other people is paramount to our success. Everyone that comes into our life is an opportunity to either give love, or take it away. Every time we meet with someone, we have the chance to be abundant in love or hold back in lack and fear. What we give out, we get back. People are put in our life, to train us to choose love, to choose abundance, to choose kindness, at the heart of the situation. The more someone rejects us, responds with fear, challenges us or in any way tests us, they are just training us to show love as the main motive. The more you're being chiseled and refined, the better we'll be able to choose love in tough situations.

You will only ever be as successful as your capacity to love. I say to people all the time, if you aren't as successful as you want to be, give more love. The more you genuinely help people change their lives, the more your life will change in the process. The more we embody love, the more we are operating closer to the way we were made. If God is Love, and we are literally made in His image, that means that we are also Love. The greatest act of love that I believe that we can give someone is to wholeheartedly believe in them. It's the greatest gift you can give. It's the most priceless gift we can give in the world is to believe in someone and what's possible for them. So, are you speaking life over people? Or a speaking death over people? Are you literally bringing their dreams and goals to life, or are you crushing them and taking them away from them? Because when we take something away from someone else, it's because we've had it taken away from us in the past.

I challenge you to breathe life, possibility and light over people. Love on everyone and anyone no matter what.

Sometimes the most loving thing we can say to someone is to encourage them to go for it. So often, when we tell people that we care about, what we want to do, or what we want to create, they may attempt to hold you back. They might say, "Oh no, don't do that. It's not safe. You'd better not." While that may be coming from a place of love, it is also weighted with fear. I want you to come from a place of love and possibility as the overlay. I want you to see what's possible for people and breathe life into them. Because everyone is wanting to move forward. Everyone's wanting to accomplish things and move closer towards their goals in life. So many people are watching you too. You can be a huge beacon of possibility, whether that is to your team, your spouse, your children, everyone is on the sideline watching you play on the field. It's up to you to be that beacon of what's possible.

It is your birthright to believe in yourself. But it's your responsibility to believe in others and to spread that belief to others. There is no better feeling in the world than having the honor to believe in someone. However, there is nothing better than the privilege of having someone believe in you. When we have someone who believes in us, and when we believe in ourselves and we go for our dreams, it really allows us to experience life and experience things closer to our truest, highest, grandest vision we hold for ourselves.

So, when you meet people in life and realize they might be struggling or uneasy, I want you to think,

"How can I believe in this person right now? Is it because they feel stuck? How can I help them step into their power and actually go after what they want and create an amazing life?"

These are the times when we are challenged so we can always learn to give love to others, especially to those that don't think they are worthy of it. Because you know what? Love isn't optional. It's a commandment. Love is also the magnet of everything you desire. We are the law of attraction. When we love others, others love us. When we judge others, others judge us. It's the people that feel as if they deserve it the least that need it the most. They are just people that are placed in our path to help us to live and fill up our ability to love and believe in them. Encourage others through your kindness and love and it will always have a ripple effect. Your love will be like a pebble in a pond that ripples out support, encouragement, belief, and gratitude. All of your feelings towards others will come back multiplied to you, enhancing both your lives.

Look for the good in your relationships, look for the good in your team, look for the good in your life. Look for the good in your health and contribution. Instead of looking for what's going wrong, you already know this trip for success. Look for GREEN. Look for the good. Look for the wins. Look for the miracles. Look for the things that you want to see more of and celebrate the things you want. What if you started to treat yourself like you are worthy to receive love from all the people you know?

You want to supersize what you want because playing small doesn't serve the world. I want you to keep thinking, "What am I willing to give up to go to the next level?" Are you willing to see good instead of negative? Are you willing to speak the language of growth and abundance? What do you really need in order to believe in yourself? Identify what you need to shift your mindset into believing in yourself because we can all exercise rock-solid belief if we *truly* desire something.

I always say, "I can teach you to cook, but I can't teach you to be hungry." You've got to find that hunger for your vision and your mission. You have a gift to give back to the world, a skill that you want to sharpen. I want you to find out what that zone of genius is for you and what areas you need to increase your level of belief in. Be around people that believe in themselves. If they don't, your number one job is to believe in them first.

Think of one person that you can show love to today and reach out to them. Afterwards, write about how it made you feel.

What areas of life can you show yourself more love?

The more you can love on you the more your cup is full to be able to love on others.

You will only ever be as successful as your capacity to love.

28

YOUR VULNERABILITY
IS YOUR X-FACTOR

It's a common belief that vulnerability is a weakness. What many people don't understand is that vulnerability can be your X-Factor. However, it can be difficult for us at times to be vulnerable, I genuinely believe that vulnerability is what sets us free. It allows us to ask for what we want, go after our desires, speak our truth, and it gives us permission to absolutely be, do, and have what we want.

Sometimes being vulnerable is scary, but one thing I know is that the best place to practice being vulnerable is in the presence of love. Sometimes, when surrounded by a lack of love and support, we might begin to resent our goals if we feel as if they are not going anywhere. This ultimately leads to complaining. I've always been one to say if I'm complaining about something, it's because somewhere in the past, I didn't speak my truth. I wasn't vulnerable enough to say what I wanted, to own what I wanted, and let my desires be heard.

I know that giving yourself permission to be vulnerable may seem like a big permission slip, but, it is absolutely liberating. The best way to become vulnerable is practicing in the presence of a loving person. When we have someone we trust around us, or we speak to someone that we feel safe with, it gives us permission to be seen and truly heard. That gives us permission to be our authentic selves. In all things, being vulnerable is the gateway to connection. When we hold back what we truly want and are always scared to say what we want, we ultimately rob ourselves of life. Refusing to be vulnerable is a way of holding ourselves back from true connection.

Pure vulnerability is something that can be felt when you're only truly wholeheartedly present. When we're not wholeheartedly present and we're thinking about the past or the future, we miss out on the moment. Being vulnerable is one of the hardest things for someone to do because it's actually exposing your true self. We, as humans, are so scared of being rejected or abandoned for who we truly are. We feel the need to have the perfect hair, the perfect makeup, the perfect car, the perfect house, and all the other things we use to mask up to keep others at arm's length so that they can never truly see who we are. When we do that, it's evidence that we crave connection. When we crave connection, it's evidence that it is lacking. I encourage you to find someone you trust and be vulnerable with them. Only then can you take the shackles off. I think you genuinely cannot say the wrong thing to the right person if you're held in a space of love, and both people are coming from the same place.

Life is too short to not truly go after what you want. I think it's so amazing that we are all creators of our own future. We can create anything that we desire, and we can attract anything we want. But I really do feel that if we aren't vulnerable enough to express what we want, we won't go for it. The answer will always, be no.

You've heard the saying, "When opportunity knocks, open the door." But sometimes we've got to open the door first so that opportunity can find us. That's really how you discover your power. Some of the best moments of my life have come from being honest with my true self and being vulnerable. Remember that you've got nothing to lose and everything to gain from the practice of speaking from your heart, not holding back, and not worrying what other people think of you. I think being vulnerable with others is the most loving thing that you can do besides believing in them. I think it's our time to express our vulnerability to the world and go for what we want.

Being vulnerable and authentic will give you the most incredible feeling, the feeling we are all striving for. The feeling of experiencing the present moment. The past is gone, the future is unwritten, and all we have is this moment now, and now, now, now. Here right now, is all we have and is all that exists, Be here now in whatever you are doing. Be present. Be wholeheartedly present.

Identify a close confidant that you can be vulnerable with.

Share a dream or goal with them today.

Pick up the phone and forgive, ask for forgiveness or speak your truth on a matter.

Do something today that scares you! I promise it will shift everything and the game will change! The game that is your LIFE!

Wholeheartedly present!

29

THE POWER OF YOUR RELATIONSHIPS

Throughout my time as a teacher and educator I have spoken a great deal about relationships. I believe that we can create the relationships that we desire, based on the relationship that we have with ourselves. So many times, I feel that we are looking externally for answers to the relationships that we want. However, they all begin and end within. So, my question to you is, what sort of relationship do you have with yourself? Are you looking for the good in yourself each day? Are you speaking life over yourself each day? What are the things that you say to yourself that allow you to really become your own best friend?

If there's one person that has your back in this life and on this planet, it's you. It has to be you. Your relationships are all going to be mirrors of the way that you treat yourself and the way that you look after and love yourself first. So first of all, what are you speaking? What are you affirming? Are you affirming that you're a great leader? Are you affirming that you are a great mother, sister, father, brother, son, helper, or community neighbor? What are you affirming to yourself? Are you saying that you're good at what you do, and that you're getting better every day?

One of the affirmations that I use is, *"Every day in every way, I'm getting better and better."* That gives me permission to be learning and growing. I do understand that sometimes we fail and sometimes we fall down, but these are all steps in the process. Some days we fail, and on others, we succeed. Whether I'm having a good or bad day, that affirmation has given me compassion for myself to allow myself to always be growing and getting better at what I do. You have to give yourself the grace to speak life.

Take note of what your desires are for your relationships and see how you are embodying them yourself. Ask how you are being kind, compassionate, excited, graceful, fun, enthusiastic, and supportive of yourself. Are you backing yourself and your goals and dreams? Are you backing yourself in the vision you hold for yourself? Are you looking after yourself by having people around you that support you and love you and lift you up?

Become familiar with the feeling associated with having a really supportive friend. Ask yourself how it feels when you have a really good, open, vulnerable, connected conversation with someone. How does it feel when you feel supported and heard? Do you allow space for yourself to do that?

Your journal can be your best friend in moments like these. You can get your journal out and you can ask yourself, "Who am I wanting to be today? How does that feel? What am I going through today? What do I need to say if I was my best friend sitting across from me at a table having a coffee? What would I say to myself today?"

In order to be the best version of yourself for the greater good of all those around you in your life, memorize the feelings associated with being your Ideal Self. Journal out those key feelings and live by them. I recommend that you write down the things that you love and want to say about yourself–the things that you'd say to your best friend. If you don't really know what you need to say, imagine if your best friend was sitting across from you. I make it a point to tell myself,

I believe in you. I trust you and I know the best things are working out for you. You've got this and you're deserving of your greatest, highest good. I can absolutely see the path that you're destined to be on, and I believe that you can absolutely have it all. I know your destination is exactly what you're holding in your mind. Go out there and claim it for yourself. I believe in you and your capabilities.

I want to challenge you to raise your expectation of what you want and how you expect to be treated. Starting with yourself first is key. When you have things you want from your family, friends, and team, start by looking inwards. When we are developing ourselves for the sake of our relationships, we're also more likely to look for the good and assume the best intentions. It will free you from thinking anything negative about other people.

Your relationships are one of the keys to believing. When you have a good relationship with yourself, that ripples out to those around you. When you create a circle of those that believe in you, you start to believe in yourself more. The best part is, your relationships are something that you can enhance every day, starting from within.

Practice some self-talk and have a conversation with yourself as if you were your own best friend. Identify some qualities that you search for in your relationships, then see how you can work on them within yourself.

Stand in the mirror and talk it out while looking deeply into your own eyes.

Every day in every way, I'm getting better and better…

30
ARE YOU COMMITTED
TO BELIEVING?

How committed are you to what you want? Since I've already taught you how to see what you want and identify the feelings associated with it, your next step is to showcase those things in a vision and keep it on your mind. Affirm it, set a deadline to it, treat it with urgency, and get into massive, aligned action to create that incredible vision. It's up to you. It starts now. It's going to come down to how committed you are. Commitment is one of my favorite things, as it helps us identify the things that we do, say and represent throughout the day. It's about whether we say "yes" or "no" to things.

One of the things I'm committed to is living a magnificent life, in all areas. I make choices and decisions based on that becoming a reality. So, when someone offers me something, or I get invited somewhere, or an opportunity comes up, I ask, "is this taking me closer or further away from that end vision of that magnificent life?" That's something I want you to ask yourself from now on too.

We all have big goals, and I want you to know that it's up to you to keep the commitment to those dreams for yourself. No one else will commit to what you want more than you.

It's something that we have to hold onto. Commitment is powerful. It's putting a stake in the ground signifying that it's done. Ask yourself, are you really committed to living an awesome life? Are you committed to living the highest, truest, grandest vision you hold for yourself? Are you committed to beginning now? Boldness has genius, power, and magic in it. Knowing what you want and saying "yes" to your desires is absolute boldness because most people go through life being pushed around by people, places, and things. They end up in their day, week, month, and year going,

"I don't really know what happened."

Treat your life as if you are a curator. Determine what sort of story you are writing. Are you writing a fantastic story of hope? One of knowing, faith, trust, and belief? Or are you writing a story of doubt, fear, rejection and scarcity? Write yourself a fantastic story. Believe in yourself and know that you're worthy and deserving of it.

Commitment is really what sets you apart from the rest. Most people find it hard to commit. They may know what they want, but they just will not commit to it. When you are afraid to commit, I want you to ask yourself,

"Why not me?"

Why not you to have it all? Why not live that epic vision for yourself? I know that you deserve it. I know that you can have it. You know it too. You've got to take on a mentality of saying "If it's meant to be, it's absolutely up to me." There's nothing that can get in the way of a committed mind and heart. Find the courage to put your word to something and you say, "This is me. This is who I am. This is what I'm creating," that is when the world steps aside. The world steps aside for someone who knows where they're going.

I want you to have a fierce desire in your heart and a fierce knowing that everything you want is all yours. It's up to you to claim it though. It's up to you to have the confidence to go after it. There's nothing out there that is not possible. If you put a commitment out there in any area of your life and put the work in, you're going to have it. It's absolutely yours. Behind every strong, independent person stands someone who had to learn how to stand up in the beginning. You've got to learn to stand up and not depend on others, but instead be the inspiration for others. Just like self-belief, your level of commitment is contagious. Others seeing you going all-out for your goals will spur them to do the same.

That is the power of commitment, my friends. That is what comes when you burn the boats. That is what happens when you decide to slam that back door. You will make other people want to rise. You will help people stop surviving and start thriving. You will help people stop numbing and start living. You will help people go from mediocrity to magnificence because you've made a commitment to be a beacon of light to show other people what's possible. You're going to show everyone that you're not going to let anything get in the way.

Be relentless. Dare to be unrealistic. Remain rock-solid in your faith and your knowing, and trust in yourself. Go for the ultimate vision you can imagine. When what you want is so big, you have to be courageous to go and ask for it. But guess what? If you don't ask, the answer's always no. If you knock on a door, expect it to open. If it doesn't open exactly to what you want, then go forward with the confidence that the next door might hide exactly what you're dreaming of.

Why settle for anything less than extraordinary? It's time to believe as you have never before in your life. Finishing this book is closing the last chapter of the old you. Today you walk into life with a whole suite of thirty-one skills, tips, strategies, laws, lessons, and learnings on how to change your life to live that truest, highest, grandest vision you hold for yourself. You have now learned all the ways to enhance your believing. Life from this moment on will be so different. It will be one created by you. It's true, my friends, you can have it all. Are you ready to live a life of belief? It's all possible because everything you want is on the other side of BELIEVING! Just know that wherever you go on this earth, whatever you are doing, or whatever you are experiencing, there is this bright unstoppable flame that burns inside of you, and that's my belief in YOU!

It is with you everywhere at all times.

I love you, and I BELIEVE in you!

Write down a major goal you have and stick to it. Chart your progress in your journal along the way.

The greatest commitment you will EVER make is to be totally and utterly committed to BELIEVING in yourself.

31

ACT AS IF...

At long last, we've reached the end, not of the whole voyage, but just this first journey together, the first of many to come, so stay tuned. I truly hope you have loved taking this journey towards believing in yourself as much as I have adored taking you on it. You now know all of the secrets to absolutely believing that you are worthy and deserving of having it all and living out your truest, highest vision for yourself and your life. The key now is to implement each step along the way. The more you practice each step, the more you will continue to grow in the habit of believing in yourself daily. This is what makes anything possible.

You should be incredibly proud of all that you have learned, the degree to which you have grown, and the journey you now find yourself on. Take a moment to think back on everything you've done so far and know that you are well on your way to your destination.

Everything you want is on the other side of believing.

Now, all that's left to do is "act as if."

A final factor that has delivered me to the level of success I experience today is the fact that I "acted as if" long before I arrived. Years before I was where I am now, I would ask myself, "What would Future Cass do? What would my mentors and role models do in this situation?" so I could emulate what I saw in my mind's eye. I welcome you to do the same with the mentors in your life. You can even ask yourself "What would Cass do?" if you want. I won't mind, and I'm certain you have an idea of what I might say based on our time together. The key is to emulate whoever is at the level where you aspire to be. You have a responsibility now to "act as if," because your goals are already accomplished. What you say, what you think, what you write, and what you feel will always come into reality.

At the beginning of our journey, I let you in on my little secret impromptu solo dance parties to celebrate my goals. I strongly recommend you get in on the trend, because I know the moment you decide to leap up and get excited for everything that is ahead of you, things will fall into place. As soon as you've turned the last page of this book, my hope is that you'll have your own all-out dance party, celebrating that your dreams are done, complete, and yours.

So, to return one final time to the riverbank and the celebration across the water, act as if you've already made it across. Act as if you are right in the middle of the celebration party. Carry those feelings with you always, because those are what will see you through to your destination. As you walk through life, my hope is that you will see that all things are working in your favor. I believe that the most loving thing you can do for someone is to believe in them, and I hope you know from the bottom of my heart that I love you and I believe in you.

Believe, because if I can, you can.

What did you love most about reading this book?

What are you most proud of during your time reading?

What is a favorite tool you learned that you will take with you throughout your life?

Tag me, share your feelings, ah-ha moments, and breakthroughs @cassandrahouse_ or connect@cassandrahouse.com

I AM your human sized permission slip to BELIEVE in YOURSELF!

I grant you full and complete permission to radically BELIEVE in YOU!

AFFIRMATIONS

Here are some affirmations you can add to your vision board:

- I create a reality where...
- There is an infinite amount of everything I want and need.
- I radiate beauty, charm, and grace.
- Whatever I put my mind to, I can achieve.
- I choose friends, conversations, and situations that encourage me to play big.
- The perfect relationship for me is coming into my life sooner than I expect.
- I am the designer of my life; I build its foundation and choose its contents.
- Today, I am brimming with energy and overflowing with joy.
- I wake up today with strength in my heart and clarity in my mind.
- My obstacles are moving out of my way; my path is carved towards greatness.
- My business is growing, expanding, and thriving.

- Many people look up to me and recognize my worth; I am admired.
- I am at peace with all that has happened, is happening, and will happen.
- I am blessed with an incredible family and wonderful friends.
- I constantly attract opportunities that create more prosperity in my life.
- My thoughts are filled with positivity, possibility, and self-love.
- Love, joy, and abundance are suddenly within my grasp.
- My goals are becoming a reality today.
- I feel light, blissful, and enlightened; I know that anything is possible.
- Nothing matters and everything is amazing.
- I have continual feelings of safety, love, acceptance and belonging.
- I create positive habits daily.
- Happiness is a choice. I base my happiness on my own accomplishments and the blessings I've been given.
- No outside force is responsible for my joy.
- I am courageous and I stand up for myself.
- A river of compassion washes over me and replaces all with love.
- I appreciate each moment of the day.

- I am grateful for all things, people, and situations; I allow them all to serve me as I abundantly serve them.

- Creative energy surges through me and leads me to new and brilliant ideas.

- I have been given endless talents which I begin to utilize today.

- I am superior to negative thoughts, small conversations and low actions.

- I possess the qualities needed to be extremely successful.

- I expand my awareness of the abundance around me.

- My body is healthy, my mind is brilliant, and my soul is tranquil.

- Abundance is my basic nature.

- I give and receive prosperity with heart.

- I am filled with great abundance now.

- I create wealth easily and effortlessly.

- There is abundance everywhere I go.

- I am deserving, worthy, and enough to attract anything I want and need into my life.

- I am powerful beyond measure and nothing or no one affects my state of mind.

- I was born to be prosperous.

- I live life abundantly.

- I am capable and excel in any area I put my mind to.

- I am the epitome of success.

- I choose to be successful, and I believe I can have it all.

- I love myself and I am loved by others.

- I love unconditionally.

- I attract confident, coachable, hardworking, independent leaders who are kind, loving, and ready for success.

- I attract into my life people that bring out the best in me.

- I am a great leader with the perfect balance of community and contribution.

- Integrity and authenticity are what I'm known for.

- I connect with myself before connecting with others.

- I exhibit a consistent mood and maintain an optimistic attitude.

- I have a culture that balances contribution, community, responsibility, and accountability.

LET'S MONETIZE YOUR GENIUS AND WORK TOGETHER AT CASSANDRA HOUSE INTERNATIONAL

I coach people around the globe through the motions of 'Monetizing their Genius' and taking that inner genius to market. I help people turn their passion into a business or a course so they can scale their genius to the world, turn it into a profitable business, and get paid to do what they love! I love seeing people be their own boss, build their own empire instead of someone else's, and be empowered to believe that anything is possible. I love seeing people have that new lease on life to do what they love with whom they love anywhere in the world. I help people do this without waiting for the perfect time or after having for decades building someone else's empire while leaving their dreams on the shelf. Not any longer; that stops today! YOU deserve to live the truest, highest, grandest vision you hold for yourself NOW! Why wait? I am here to be your human-sized permission slip to believe in yourself, so you don't have to have any more doubt, fear, or uncertainty about how you will do it because I'm here to show you how and hold your hand every step of the way!

As my journey to success has progressed, I have helped many people like you become impactful coaches, create hugely successful courses, build thriving global businesses, become passionate authors, leave 9-5 and become a successful entrepreneurs in their own right and work with world-class inventors, all in releasing their geniuses to the world. I love seeing people's genius in the pages of their first book, within a scaleable course of their own, in the product they have created going to market, designing their own online business, or by changing lives working with people they coach. My passion and forte are mentoring people to step into their power, own their greatness, and be absolutely in love with their life, career, and self. My first business card at 18 said "Creating opportunities for others" and "Changing lives, one incredible person at a time." It still says this to this day. I didn't realize back then how my purpose was already at the forefront of everything I was doing, and now with two decades of experience and success, I'm ready more than ever to serve you and give what I know over to you. My soul's purpose is to create opportunities for others, to believe in and empower them to say yes to the opportunity to live their dream life and make it their reality today!

I'm all about showing people by mentoring them to achieve the success they deeply desire through teaching "Life and Success" and "Leadership and Business Mastery." I can transform your belief systems so you can go from where you are to where you want to be in my Empowered Women's Collective, my Genius Inner Circle, or my Genius Millionaire Mastermind, one of the Crown Jewels of my offerings.

I have always believed in no one missing out, so I genuinely have something for all walks of life, commitment levels, and investment points. All are welcome, even for newbies with no experience who want to learn to expert entrepreneurs who wish to master their next level of life in every facet there is. So, whether big or small, there's something for you! Learn how to MONETIZE YOUR GENIUS, Your Idea, Product, Passion, or Personal Brand by following a simple blueprint for success that can generate 6 and 7 figures for you like it has many around the globe. I'm ready to guide you and teach you all I have learned and know in 20 years of business, leadership, and success.

I am here to hold your hand and take you through the motions of taking your genius to market. To empower you beyond belief and to mentor you to live the truest, highest.grandest, vision you hold for yourself. Believe: If I Can, You Can.

Join me at Cassandra House International by applying for the following:

CREATE YOUR COURSE
BECOME A CERTIFIED COACH
EMPOWERED WOMEN COLLECTIVE
GENIUS INNER CIRCLE
GENIUS MILLIONAIRE MASTERMIND
BE MENTORED BY CASSANDRA
WRITE YOUR BOOK
RELEASE YOUR INVENTION

Create your dream life with me!

For all offers, speaking engagements,
and media bookings, visit:

Cassandra House International
www.cassandrahouse.com